JOHN SADLER & ROSIE SERDIVILLE

TOMMY ROT

WWI POETRY
THEY DIDN'T
LET YOU READ

This one is for all of them

First published 2013

The History Press
The Mill, Brimscombe Port
Stroud, Gloucestershire, GL5 2QG
www.thehistorypress.co.uk

British Library Cataloguing in Publication Data.
A catalogue record for this book is available from the British Library.

ISBN 978 0 7524 9208 7

Typesetting and origination by The History Press
Printed in Great Britain

CONTENTS

At every Great War memorial service, the soldier is referred to as though patriotism had been the chief influence that had made him join the army and ultimately die in action. To the ex-serviceman who has had his eyes opened to the lies and deceptions of the Great War, how sad and ignorant it all is, he knows that practically all the pious outpourings over their dead comrades and comrades enemies are based on a false thesis.

The majority of the rank and file of the 'Contemptibles' joined the army for many various reasons other than that of patriotism; unemployment, home troubles and petty evils were the best recruiting sergeants in pre-war days and, when the war came, the spirit of adventure was the main influence, backed by every possible means of enticement and coercion. If the psychology of the un-conscripted Great War British soldier could ever be written, patriotism would be the least of impulses and hard instinct of men of fighting temperament at the top.

The truth about the non-commissioned soldier, who fought in the Great War, is a thing to be ashamed of, instead of being blessed and glorified as a virtue by those who are far removed from the foul realities of it.

Sergeant Charles H. Moss, 18th (Pals) Battalion,
Durham Light Infantry, *c.* 1924

Acknowledgements

This book could not have been written without the generous assistance of a number of organisations and individuals and our particular thanks are due to: Roberta Goldwater of *A Soldier's Life* and colleagues at Tyne and Wear Archives and Museums; Ian Martin of the King's Own Scottish Borderers Museum, Berwick-upon-Tweed; the Trustees of the Green Howards Museum, Richmond; the Trustees of the Durham Light Infantry Museum and Art Gallery; the staff of Durham County Record Office; the staff of Northumberland County Archives at Woodhorn; the Trustees of the Fusiliers Museum of Northumberland, Alnwick; to colleagues at the North East Centre for Lifelong Learning at the University of Sunderland; staff at the Literary and Philosophical Library, Newcastle; staff at Central Libraries, Newcastle and Gateshead, Clayport Library Durham, Northumberland Libraries at Morpeth, Alnwick, Blyth, Hexham and Cramlington; Lindsey and Colin Durward of Blyth Battery, Blyth, Northumberland; Amy Cameron of the National Army Museum; the curator and staff of the Royal Engineers Museum, Library and Archive, Chatham; Tony Ball of the Western Front Association; Jennifer Laidler and Samantha Kelly for original verse; and to Morag Miller and family. In particular, Gerry

Tomlinson has been a source of immense support and stimulation. Special thanks are due to editorial colleagues at The History Press for another successful collaboration.

As ever, the authors remain responsible for all errors and omissions.

Rosie Serdiville & John Sadler, Northumberland, January 2013

INTRODUCTION

Charles Hamilton Sorley (1895–1915) had been studying German at Jena for six months when war broke out. The Scot immediately joined up and, serving with the Suffolk Regiment, he had reached the rank of Captain when he was killed during the Battle of Loos at the age of 20. His final poem was discovered in the kit bag attached to his lifeless body. Sassoon and Masefield maintained that he would have taken his place amongst the greatest war poets had he lived.

TO GERMANY

You are blind like us. Your hurt no man designed,
And no man claimed the conquest of your land.
But, gropers both through fields of thought confined,
We stumble and we do not understand.
You only saw your future bigly planned,
And we, the tapering paths of our own mind,
And in each other's dearest ways we stand,
And hiss and hate. And the blind fight the blind.

When it is peace, then we may view again
With never-won eyes each other's truer form,
And wonder. Grown more loving-kind and warm,
We'll grasp firm hands and laugh at the old pain,
When it is peace. But, until peace, the storm,
The darkness, and the thunder and the rain.

Charles Hamilton Sorley

On the sultry afternoon of 28 June 1914, an 18-year-old terrorist shot Archduke Franz Ferdinand and his wife outside a pavement café in the Bosnian city of Sarajevo. Few in Britain at that time had heard of the Duke, the city or the province and, for the most part, cared rather less; just another 'Balkan do'. It wasn't. This was the spark that lit the world, blowing the fuse that consumed the great empires and dynasties of Europe. Austria-Hungary, Germany, Russia and Turkey would be blown clear away. Britons were swept up in a tidal wave of righteous sentiment; the beastly Hun had to be stopped and gallant little Belgium restored. No other nation sustained its war effort relying solely upon volunteers. The stern, commanding face of Herbert Kitchener let every man know what path duty demanded he take. Nobody had any real inkling, except perhaps the general himself, of what consequences would follow. It was all about the glorious crusade.

AN EXTRACT FROM VICTORY DAY –
ANTICIPATION

As sure as God's in his heaven,
As sure as he stands for right,
As sure as the Hun this wrong hath done,
So surely we win this fight!

Then! –
Then, the visioned eye shall see
The great and noble company,
That gathers there from land and sea,
From over-land and over-sea,
From under-land and under-sea,
To celebrate right royally
The Day of Victory

Not alone on that great day
Will the war-worn victors come,
To meet our great glad 'Welcome Home'!
And a whole world's deep 'Well done'!
Not alone! Not alone will they come,
To the sound of the pipe and the drum;
They will come to their own
With the pipe and the drum,
With the merry, merry tune
Of the pipe and the drum; -
But-they-will-not-come-alone!

John Oxenham

These noble, desperately naïve posturings would not endure. The conflict that 'would be over by Christmas' dragged through numerous Christmases to consume blood and treasure at a rate undreamed of. For the British, however, the idea of conscription was anathema: free men enlisted because it was right, not because the state compelled. Never before in history, and probably never again, was the road to war so heavily subscribed.

NO CONSCRIPTION

Would you show your love for freedom?
Would you stand for truth and right?
Would you take the path of wisdom?
Then be ready for the fight!

[Chorus]

For we won't have conscription,
We all hate conscription,
We don't want conscription
So we'll all be volunteers.

Would you keep your homes in safety?
And protect the fatherland?
Have your commerce prosper greatly,
On the sea and on the land

[Chorus]

Have we foes across the water?
Who must be kept at bay?
If we value freedom's charter,
We'll be ready e-en than they.

[Chorus]

But should the foe ever threaten,
Or but touch our silver strand,
We will drown him in the ocean,
By the aid of God's right hand!

[Chorus]

For gold the merchant ploughs the main;
The farmer ploughs the manor;
But glory is the soldier's prize,
The soldier's wealth is honour.
The brave, fair soldier ne'er despise,
Nor count him as a stranger
Remember, he's his country's stay
In day and hour of danger!

'Bobby' Burns, 11 February 1917

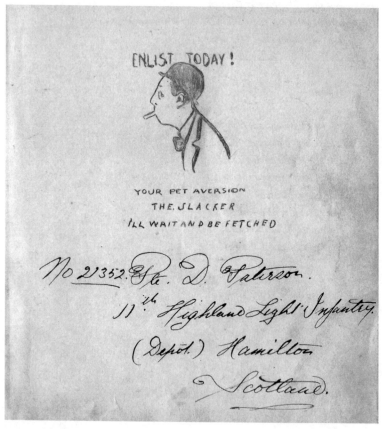

Enlist today. (Author's own)

The editor of In Flanders Fields quotes Edward Thomas when he observes that war poetry does not generally endure. Despite our seemingly endless fascination with the Great War poets, this remains true. How many of us have heard of Colwyn Erasmus Arnold Phillips (1888–1915)? He was killed in action at the age of 26 and his poem, 'Release', was found in his kit bag when his belongings were sent home:

There is a healing magic in the night,
The breeze blows cleaner than it did by day,
Forgot the fever of the fuller light,
And sorrow sinks insensibly away
As if some saint a cool white hand did lay
Upon the brow, and calm the restless brain.
The moon looks down with pale unpassioned ray
Sufficient for the hour is its pain.
Be still and feel the night that hides away earth's stain.
Be still and loose the sense of God in you,
Be still and send your soul into the all,
The vasty distance where the stars shine blue,
No longer antlike on the earth to crawl.
Released from time and sense of great or small,
Float on the pinions of the Night-Queen's wings;
Soar till the swift inevitable fall
Will drag you back into all the world's small things;
Yet for an hour be one with all escaped things.

Colwyn Phillips

His brother, Roland, was killed just over a year later in July 1916, also at the age of 26. Colwyn was a racing enthusiast, and here he compares war to racing:

RACING RHYMES

HAVE you felt the joy that is almost fear
As you face the ditch and are two lengths clear,
And you hear the thunder of hoofs in rear?
There is just a second when you may see
Clear out what the consequence will be
If you go too close or take off too far
Comes a rending crash and a sickening jar,
A futile arm that you raise to defend,
And the battering hoofs that bring the end.

You are stride for stride, and you set your lip
As you urge with your heel and raise your whip,
And the moment he feels the whipcord sting
He leaps from the track with a glorious spring.
You hear the crash as the stout birch sunders,
And gain a length as your rival blunders.

Colwyn Phillips

1

1914: EXPECTATION

Industrial warfare dawned as a crusade; noble, chivalric, Homeric. The reality was to prove very different. You can tell this was written before the cold reality had become apparent.

SHALL WE FORGET THEM?

Shall we forget them?
They who marched with smiles away,
When dawned the long-expected day,
Of German making
High were their heads and firm their lips,
As they trod the street to the waiting ships,
Then eastwards taking.

Shall we forget them?
Men of blood who gave up life
In a noble cause in day of strife,
And to glory trod.
Or, in the days to come shall our children tell
The story of those who fighting fell?
For England and for God!

J. Cooke

Haldane's reforms earlier in the new century had swept away the old militia system in favour of the modern pattern of Territorials. Kitchener was not a fan. His own experience when serving as a volunteer with the French equivalent in the Franco-Prussian War of 1870–71 had, quite wrongly, led to mistrust. One of the first Territorial units to serve in the Great War, thrown into the cauldron of First Ypres, was the Northumberland Hussars; a former yeomanry (cavalry) regiment with indelible links to their home county and known, affectionately, as the 'Noodles'.

THE NOODLE AN' RIFLEMAN'S DISPUTE

The Noodles thor a' gentlemen,
Respected to be sure,
They nivor like the rifle curs,
Fixed ramrods of the Moor; the riflemen black-legged us a',
Undermined wor daily pay,
But smash, aw'll fight him for a quart
Then for war lads, clear the way.

Joe Wilson

With the Noodles went Peter the cat, their somewhat grumpy mascot, who was handed over as they set off for France. The war did nothing for Peter's humour and he rightly refused to ever alight from his privileged perch atop the ration cart. He did, however, survive the war and came safe home to medals and a gentlemanly retirement, although not with any evident good grace!

SPIRIT OF THE NEW ARMY

Fear death?
I would hate that death bandaged my eyes and forbore
And bade me creep past,
No! Let me taste the whole of it, fare like my peers
The heroes of old,
Bear the brunt, in a minute pay gladly life's arrears,
Of pain and darkness and cold;
For sudden the worst turns the best to the brave,
The black minute's at end
And the elements rage, the fiend-voices that rage
Shall dwindle, shall blend,
Small change shall become first a peace out of pain
Then a light ...

Anon.

Adulation for those in khaki and white feathers for those without: like most enthusiasms, the passion for feathers was transient and the seemingly endless casualty lists published daily in the press soon sapped public ardour. Meanwhile, the Kaiser, with the real and imagined atrocities of his forces blazoned across the press and subject to 'spin', became a caricature.

An Interview. (Drawing in autograph book, 1914–18, author's own)

I VILL SEND OUT ULTIMATUMS

Is there anyone I've forgot?
Kaiser Wilhelm said to his Chancellor one day,
I have got a new game I'm going to play,
I am de best ruler in de world today
I vill send out ultimatums!

Of course I vill be ruler of every land
Almighty Gott is my second-in-command
When I go to heaven, he vill sit on my right hand,
Or I vill send him an ultimatum!

Anon.

On Tyneside, as in other industrial centres with large Scottish and Irish contingents, volunteers formed units which reflected their own native tradition. This was not always popular with the high command, fearful of ethnic dissent.

THE CALL OF THE PIPES

The Fiery cross is out, now
There's a beacon on each hill,
The Scottish pipes are sounding,
'Tis the slogan wild and shrill.

Anon.

A healthy dash of cynicism would often follow the dire realities of industrial warfare.

I heard the bugles callin' an' join I felt I must,
Now I wish I'd let them go on blowin' till they bust!

Anon.

When Herbert Waugh, a young volunteer with the 'Tyneside Commercials' who was blooded and wounded at St Julien in 1915, finally returned from war, he would be sounding an altogether more sombre note:

Do you remember (you at the street corner or you in your private office), the thaw near Peronne which turned dry trenches into miniature canals, the march up to Arras in the snow, when someone burst a blood vessel and died by the roadside, the promulgation of a court martial before daybreak near a Belgian farmhouse, followed by a volley in the next field and, within two hours, a newly filled grave in the field beyond.

Do you remember that peculiar smell which had only one meaning; the miles of duckboard track, with horrid caricatures floating in the slime beneath? Do you remember the March retreat in 1917 when the unit strolled thirty miles across country in seven days, half asleep, defending a road here and a wood there? Do you remember when, on one parade, the battalion numbered two officers and less than 20 men, when the French shot some of us (quite by accident) and our own gunners (again by accident) shot others?

Disillusionment was for the future. In 1914 it was all about the good fight:

WOR CONTEMPTIBLE BRITISH ARMY

Three cheers for wor brave Tommies, wherever they may be,
Likewise to wor allies which lie beyond the seas;
They've fitten well together, nyen kin that deny
They went away determined, to conquer or to die.

Chas Anderson

Kipling's 'Tommy Atkins', generally despised in peacetime, was now elevated to noble stature:

THE BIG PUSH

God bless wor gallant armies, on the sea and land,
Splendid deeds they have done, we hear from every hand,
In fact there's none can beat them for stability, courage and skill,
They stand predominant above all others, I trust they always will.

Chas Anderson

Gushing, leaden sentimentality is not entirely a modern phenom-
enon; in 1919 we plunged knee deep into an ecstasy of righteous,
patriotic zeal:

THE BONNY ENGLISH ROSE

Old England's emblem is the Rose,
There is no other flower,
Hath half the graces that adorn,
The beauty of the bower:
And England's daughters are as fair
As any bud that blows
What son of hers who hath not loved
Some bonny English rose.
Who hath not heard on one sweet flower,
The first among the fair,
For whom the best of English hearts,
Have breathed a fervent prayer?
Oh, may it never be her lot
To lose that sweet repose
That peace of mind which blows now
The bonny English rose.

If any bold enough there be
To war against England's Isle,
They soon shall find for English hearts,
What charms hath woman's smile,
Thus nerved, the thunder of their guns,
Would teach aspiring foes,
How vain the power that defies
The bonny English rose!

Charles Jeffrys

Drawing of a friend – W. Moore. (Drawing in autograph book, 1914–18, author's own)

From, stern, unsmiling Kitchener, the message was rather more restrained:

You are ordered abroad as a soldier of the King to help our French comrades against the invasion of a common enemy. You have to perform a task which will need your courage, your energy, your patience. Remember that the honour of the British army depends on your individual conduct... Be invariably courteous, considerate and kind. Never do anything likely to injure or destroy property and always look upon looting as a disgraceful act.
Do your duty bravely,
Fear God,
Honour the King.

Nobody expected the war that was to follow. This was industrial war, powered by technology and waged on a scale never seen before. When Hiram Maxim asked an American friend in the 1880s how best to employ his creative talents, it was suggested he should invent new machines for mass killing so European armies could slaughter each other even more effectively. He obliged and produced the machine gun.

THE BOLD KING'S HUSSARS

The air is filled with loud hurrahs
For the bold and dashing King's Hussars,
Who on the 24th May
To fame and glory carved their way
Positions held, 'spite deadly fire
Thousands saved from a funeral pyre
'Beyond all praise' the words were true
They did as the 15th always do.
Here's a motto for all – a motto for you,
Behave as the 15th always do!

A.B. Crump

Reality was to prove very different and far less glamorous. The British Expeditionary Force (BEF) first encountered the Germans at Mons on 23 August 1914, and then again at Le Cateau three days later. After the deliverance of the Marne and the beginnings of position warfare, one last chance for the combatants to potentially outflank each other arose at Ypres. It was a name largely unknown, but one which would resonate.

I WANT TO TELL YOU NOW SIR

I want to tell you now sir
Before it's all forgot
That we were up at Wipers [Ypres]
And found it very hot

> *Plum & Apple* (magazine of the Northumberland
> Hussars), September 1915

The First Battle of Ypres raged through the autumn of 1914. The line held, but only just, and at a fearful cost. The 'Old Contemptibles' of the BEF were terribly thinned when the cold, wet and mud of Flanders closed about the survivors. From now on it was to be position warfare, with every yard of ground bitterly contested and paid for in blood.

I don't want to join the army; I don't want to go to war,
I'd rather hang around Piccadilly underground,
Living on the earnings of a high born lady

Anon.

A FEW HINTS FOR TOMMY BY 'ONE WOT KNOWS'

My son, beware the aircraft that flies above for his nose-caps return to earth as thou walkest, and if one drop near thee, though thou say 'pooh' yet shall thy feet be cold under thee.

Tread carefully the end of the duckboard in the trench, lest haply the other end rise and smite thee. Speak fair unto the ASC that when thou returnest from leave, he may give thee lifts in his Lorries.

Better Maconochie [stew] and biscuit in rest, than chicken and Moulin Rouge in the line, at a whizz-bang shalt thou shrug thy shoulders, at two thine eyebrows raise, at three shalt thou quicken thy pace, at four peradventure thou mayest run but a 'five-nine' who can stick it?

If a man say unto you 'Leave is open, leave is open' regard him not for he is a liar, and talketh through his hat (tin). Walk not upon the Decauville Track though it is the shorter way, that the wrath of the OC descend not upon thy head and he dock thy leave.

Beware the barrage that creepeth and the Minen that is Werfer that thy days may be long in the line. Verily, a sandbag is a comfortable thing, it buildeth up the parapet, it improveth the dugout and maketh warm the legs of man.

A simple soul accepteth twenty-five francs to the pound but a wise man insisteth on twenty-seven fifty and raiseth Cain till he gets it. From the unit to the field ambulance is easy, from thence to the CCS mayhap harder but from the CCS to the base hospital, who shall wangle it?

Ernest Mathers, 16th London Regiment Queen's
Westminster Rifles

There was action at sea in 1914; defeat and then victory in the South Atlantic with the battles of Coronel and the Falklands:

BATTLE OF THE FALKLAND ISLES

THE Isle Juan Fernandez off Valparaiso Bay,
'Twas there that Cradock sought
The action that he fought
For he said: 'To run from numbers is not our English way,
Nor do we question why
We are fore-ordained to die.'
Though his guns were scooping water and his tops were blind with spray.

In the red light of the sunset his ships went down in flame,
He and his brave men
Were never seen again,
And Von Spec he stroked his beard, and said: 'Those
Englishmen are game,
But their dispositions are
More glorious than war;
Those that greyhounds set on mastiffs are surely much to blame.'

Then the Board of Admiralty to Sir Doveton Sturdee said:
'Take a proper naval force
And steer a sou'west course,
And show the world that England is still a Power to dread.'
Like scorpions and whips
Was vengeance to his ships,
And Cradock's guiding spirit flew before their line ahead.

Through tropic seas they shore like a meteor through the sky,
And the dolphins in their chase
Grew weary of the race;

The swift grey-pinioned albatross behind them could not fly,
And they never paused to rest
Upon the ocean's breast
Till their southern shadows lengthened and the Southern
Cross rode high.

Then Sir Doveton Sturdee said in his flagship captain's ear:
'By yon kelp and brembasteen
'Tis the Falkland Isles, I ween,
Those mollymauks and velvet-sleeves they signal land is near,
Give your consorts all the sign
To swing out into line,
And keep good watch 'twixt ship and ship till Graf von Spee appear.'

The Germans like grey shadows came stealing round the Horn,
Or as a wolf-pack prowls
With blood upon its jowls,
Their sides were pocked with gun-shots and their guns were battle-
worn,
And their colliers down the wind
Like jackals trailed behind,
'Twas thus they met our cruisers on a bright December morn.

Like South Atlantic rollers half a mile from crest to crest,
Breaking on basalt rocks
In thunderous battle-shocks,
So our heavy British metal put their armour to the test.
And the Germans hurried north,
As our lightning issued forth,
But our battle-line closed round them like a sickle east and west.

Each ship was as a pillar of grey smoke on the sea,
Or mists upon a fen,
Till they burst forth again
From their wraiths of battle-vapour by wind and speed made free;

Three hours the action sped,
Till, plunging by the head,
The Scharnhorst drowned the pennant of Admiral von Spee.

At the end of two hours more her sister ship went down
Beneath the bubbling wave,
The Gneisenau found her grave,
And Nürnberg and Leipzig, those cities of renown,
Their cruiser god-sons, too,
Were both pierced through and through,
There was but one of all five ships our gunners did not drown.

'Twas thus that Cradock died, 'twas thus Von Spee was slain,
'Twas thus that Sturdee paid
The score those Germans made,
'Twas thus St. George's Ensign was laundered white again,
Save the Red Cross over all
The graves of those who fall,
That England as of yore may be Mistress of the Main.

I.C. Colvin

Ian Colvin (1877–1938) was a journalist and historian. Born in Inverness, the son of a Free Church Minister, he worked in India and South Africa before becoming a leading writer on the Morning Post, an ultra-conservative newspaper, in 1911. His pen name whilst working in South Africa was 'Rip van Winkle'.

GUNS AT SEA

LET me get back to the guns again,
I hear them calling me,
And all I ask is my own ship, and the surge of the open sea,
In the long, dark nights, when the stars are out, and the
clean salt breezes blow,
And the land's foul ways are half forgot, like nightmare,
and I know
That the world is good, and life worthwhile, and man's real work
to do,
In the final test, in Nature's school, to see which of us
rings true.
On shore, in peace, men cheat and lie but you can't do
that at sea,
For the sea is strong; if your work is weak, vain is the
weakling's plea
Of a 'first offence' or 'I'm only young,' or 'It shall not
happen again,'
For the sea finds out your weakness, and writes its lesson
plain.
'The liar, the slave, the slum-bred cur let them stay
ashore, say I,
'For, mark it well, if they come to me, I break them and
they die.
'The land is kind to a soul unsound; I find and probe the
flaw,
'For I am the tears of eternity that rock to eternal law.'

I love the touch of the clean salt spray on my hands and
hair and face,
I love to feel the long ship leap, when she feels the sea's
embrace,
While down below is the straining hull, o'erhead the gulls
and clouds,

*And the clean wind comes 'cross the vast sea space, and
sings its song in the shrouds.*
*But now in my dreams, besides the sounds one always
hears at sea,*
*I hear the mutter of distant guns, which call and call
to me,*
*Singing: 'Come! The day is here for which you have
waited long.'*
*And women's tears, and craven fears, are drowned in that
monstrous song.*
*So whatever the future hold in store, I feel that I must
go*
*To where, thro' the shattering roar, I hear a voice that
whispers low:*
*'The craven, the weak, the man with nerves, from me
they must keep away,*
*Or a dreadful price in shattered nerves, and broken health
they pay.*
*But send me the man who is calm and strong, in the face
of my roaring blast,*
*He shall tested be in my mighty fires, and if he shall live
at the last,*
*He can go to his home, his friends, his kin, to his life e'er
war began,*
*With a new-found soul, and a new-found strength, knowing
himself a man.'*

Imtarfa (Anon.)

The editor of The Muse in Arms, an anthology of British war poetry,
identifies 'Imtarfa' as a naval officer.

An early naval epic was the career of the German surface raider
Emden, brought to a final Götterdämmerung by HMAS Sidney. Henry
Newbolt (1862–1938) was a barrister, playwright and author.

A friend of Sir Douglas Haig, he was recruited by the War Propaganda Bureau to promote a positive view of the conflict and keep the British public on side – work that earned him a knight-hood in 1915. He was fascinated by the sea and the Navy and went on to publish two volumes of the official history of the war at sea.

A SHANTY OF THE EMDEN

The captain of the Emden
He spread his wireless net,
And told the honest British tramp
Where raiders might be met:
Where raiders might be met, my lads,
And where the coast was clear,
And there he sat like a crafty cat
And sang while they drew near
'Now you come along with me, sirs,
You come along with me!
You've had your run, old England's done,
And it's time you were home from Sea!'

The seamen of old England
They doubted his intent,
And when he hailed, 'Abandon ship!'
They asked him what he meant:
They asked him what he meant, my lads,
The pirate and his crew,
But he said, 'Stand by! your ship must die,
And it's luck you don't die too!
So you come along with me, sirs,
You come along with me:
We find our fun now yours is done,
And it's time you were home from sea!'

He took her, tramp or trader,
He sank her like a rock,
He stole her coal and sent her down
To Davy's deep-sea dock:
To Davy's deep-sea dock, my lads,
The finest craft afloat,
And as she went he still would sing
From the deck of his damned old boat
'Now you come along with me, sirs,
You come along with me:
Your good ship's done with wind and sun,
And it's time you were home from sea!'
The captain of the Sydney
He got the word by chance;
Says he, 'By all the Southern Stars,
We'll make the pirates dance:
We'll make the pirates dance, my lads,
That this mad work have made,
For no man knows how a hornpipe goes
Until the music's played.
So you come along with me, sirs,
You come along with me:
The game's not won till the rubber's done,
And it's time to be home from sea!'

The Sydney and the Emden
They went it shovel and tongs,
The Emden had her rights to prove,
The Sydney had her wrongs:
The Sydney had her wrongs, my lads,
And a crew of South Sea blues;
Their hearts were hot, and as they shot
They sang like kangaroos
'Now you come along with me, sirs,
You come along with me:

37

You've had your fun, you ruddy old Hun,
And it's time you were home from sea!'

The Sydney she was straddled,
But the Emden she was strafed,
They knocked her guns and funnels out,
They fired her fore and aft:
They fired her fore and aft, my lads,
And while the beggar burned
They salved her crew to a tune they knew,
But never had rightly learned
'Now you come along with me, sirs,
You come along with me:
We'll find you fun till the fighting's done
And the pirate's off the sea

Till the pirate's off the sea, my lads,
Till the pirate's off the sea:
We'll find them fun till the fighting's done
And the pirate's off the sea!'

Henry Newbolt

The war was not over by Christmas and the casualty lists grew longer. Despite the attrition of First Ypres, belief in the justice of the Allied cause was not yet significantly shaken. Amongst those whose fervour had not yet fled was Orlando Wright, a Northern artisan who is best remembered as a minor working-class poet. He had one published volume, *A wreath of leisure hours*, including an elegy on the Hartley Colliery Catastrophe in 1862. Much of his output is found in the newspapers of the period.

THE KAISER'S NIGHT SOLILOQUY

Hated and hiss'd by lost ones in my dream,
I wake and turn to hide me from their glare;
But midnight darkness and the morning beam
Entrench me in the horrors of despair.

What book I read has murder on its page,
And wreck and ruin proved in bloody lore;
Could clotted grief, too dense for tears, assuage
Mine should some havoc of the past restore

No green blades quiver to my fallen eye
No brooks splash music to my languid ear;
The barren landscape smokes for ever dry
With all the world upon its funeral bier.

Standing before my conscience I can feel
Its thrust divide the marrow of my should;
But worse, alas, is truth no arts conceal,
Close write and clear on Time's relentless scroll.

Oh! Mad ambition, soar no higher yet,
For, cross winds blowing, I may lower fall;
Kings can aspire to what they never get,
Or, getting nothing, think they're getting all.

Orlando Wright, *Illustrated Chronicle*, 21 August 1915

THE IRON CROSS

A thousand crosses mark the way
From town to town in Flanders fair,
The sons of Judas still betray,
And thorns of steel are everywhere.
The Iron Cross a shadow throws
Across a continent of woes.

A Man of Sorrows once endured
The paid that freed imprisoned Love,
That, by a Man of Iron's lures
Lies bleeding 'neath the bolts of Jove.
Where'er the Iron Cross ascends,
The head of love in anguish bends.

Around the sacred Cross of wood
Still shines the light of peace to be,
The conquest on that Holy Road
Is Love's eternal victory;
This passion, too, shall pass away,
Freedom shall win its Easter day.

A.W., *The Echo and Evening Chronicle* (possibly
A.W. Woodbridge, editor of the *Sunday Chronicle*
until 1925)

2

1915: RESIGNATION

W.N. Hodgson (1893–1916) is perhaps the only well-known war poet who appears in this volume. His father was the Rector of Holy Trinity Church, Berwick, until 1914. He was educated at Durham School and retained a lifelong passion for the North, particularly Cumbria. Nicknamed 'Smiler', Hodgson was awarded the Military Cross for his actions during the Battle of Loos in 1915: he held a captured trench for thirty-six hours without reinforcements or supplies. He was killed on the first day of the Somme when attacking German trenches near Mametz. Acting as bombing officer for his battalion, he was taking grenades to his comrades when a machine gun opened up. The bullet went through his neck, killing him instantly, and he was found lying next to his batman.

He wrote 'Release' while marching back after severe fighting at Loos.

RELEASE

A LEAPING wind from England,
The skies without a stain,
Clean cut against the morning
Slim poplars after rain,
The foolish noise of sparrows
And starlings in a wood
After the grime of battle
We know that these are good.

Death whining down from heaven,
Death roaring from the ground,
Death stinking in the nostril,
Death shrill in every sound,
Doubting we charged and conquered-
Hopeless we struck and stood;
Now when the fight is ended
We know that it was good.

We that have seen the strongest
Cry like a beaten child,
The sanest eyes unholy,
The cleanest hands defiled,
We that have known the heart-blood
Less than the lees of wine,
We that have seen men broken,
We know man is divine.

W.N. Hodgson

Edward Fordham Spence (1860–1932) was a solicitor and drama critic. Educated at Charterhouse, he began publishing poetry in newspapers and, three years after being called to the bar in 1890, he became a respected commentator on the theatre. His later works include: *Bar and Buskin; Being Memories of Life, Law and the Theatre* (1930); and *The Pike Fisher* (1928). He was clearly a man who appreciated his leisure activities!

COME YE APART, BE STILL

Have we forgotten to 'be still'?
Are we content to strive – until
The soul for very heaviness
Lies down to die in weariness?

Not on the field of battle is the battle won,
Not in the clash and clamour of the strife.
The heart has willed, with silent might
Alone and standing in the sight
Of God.

Where was the battle fought that issued in the cross
By him who travell'd in the greatness of his strength?
The fight was won in bitterness
The battle – in the Wilderness
Alone.

Where are the men of old who sought
The silence of the heart where thought
Is consummated by the Will?
Have we forgotten to 'be still'?

E.F. Spence, *Illustrated Chronicle*, April 1915

Imagine a saucer and the city of Ypres in the depression; around that lies a thin, barely noticeable ring of higher ground to the east and south, like a gentle rim. That is the Ypres Salient, and he who holds the rim dominates the saucer. By 1915, the Germans held this higher ground and the British position was horribly exposed, with wet, low-lying Flanders proving to be an uncomfortable and ungracious host. By the end of the First Battle of Ypres the Germans held the high ground to the east, extending to the village of Passchendaele – a name to become synonymous with horror. They also held the significant pimple of Hill 60, 2 miles south-west of the ruined city and the vital Wytschaete-Messines Ridge further south.

AN EXTRACT FROM 'THE SECOND BATTLE OF YPRES'

The streets were lined with people; it was on a Saturday,
When the local lads in their fours, to the station made their way,
It was on the seventeenth day of April, Nineteen-Fifteen,
When the band struck up that old march; 'Soldiers of the Queen'
Our ordinary drill and training was now at an end,
We had been called to the front, our country to defend.
At the station we landed, through a cheering crowd,
And the smiles on their faces proved that they were proud
Of their sons and sweethearts, of course that was us.
They had come from near and far to make this little fuss.
A guard of honour formed up, it was composed of our second line,
As we marched into the station, we thought this really fine.
And then the bugle sounded, and into the train we got,
And at 1.30 pm exactly, we were off like a shot,
We were full of excitement, some of us white,
Hardly thinking it was true that we were going to fight.
But soon this was over, and with hearts as light as cork,
It was 3.30 pm exactly when we landed in at York.
Some got on the platform, others stayed in the train,
But before many minutes we were soon off again.
Stops were made at Doncaster, Spalding, March, and then
We steamed into London Station about 10 p.m.
Things seemed a bit flurried as nearly all got out;
After such a journey we were glad to walk about.
The stay here was very short, fifteen minutes that was all.
We rushed back to the train on hearing the bugle call.
We were all fairly happy and very much alive,
When we landed at Folkestone at twelve forty-five,
From the train we walked, in silence, on to the boat,
And in less than an hour she was well afloat
Across the English Channel as quiet as could be;
We could not at any time have had a calmer sea;

There was no merriment, not even a little song;
And at 3.05 p.m. the 'Invicta' sailed into Boulogne,
In quietness we lined up in file, then in fours,
We felt a bit shaky, being on foreign shores.
The morning was very cold, and a little damp,
When we marched from the quayside to St. Martins Camp.
Here we camped till about 5.30 p.m. that night,
Then we marched to Pont de-Briques, looking fairly bright;
The journey was not heavy, just about seven miles.
We did it quite easily, amid songs and smiles.
Anyway our march was over, we had to entrain;
Our hardships had now started, it was very plain.
In cattle trucks we were packed like a lot of pigs
Hard was our position in such awful digs.
Our bones were stiff and sore, as near as I can tell,
It was about two in the morning, when we landed at Cassell.
We were shivering before we started on another tramp,
Eight miles we had to march, we could faintly hear guns rumble,
When first we heard the noise of guns, imagine if you can,
The look, the change of countenance, there was on every man;
Far away, the noise of guns seemed like rolls of thunder,
In this awful noise of death, we were going to plunder.
We halted at a French town, a place called Steenvoorde,
This is where our resting place really had to be.
We stayed here for a while, and our captains went away,
To find some likely shelter in which their men could lay;
Here the regiment then split up, each company to different farms.
We made ourselves comfortable in sheds and cattle barns,
We did not stay very long, again we had to move,
We had to get straight in the fight and our mettle prove;
Our colonel and adjutant mustered their men up to be,
Inspected before moving, by General Lindsay.
Little did some of us think, so sudden was our doom
We could not march quick enough, this was soon found out,
From foot sack to motor bus, we were roughly bumped about,

Over the rough and rocky road, the firing line got nearer,
The clash of deadly conflict was now getting clearer.
It was now getting very dark; we were well in the night,
And the flare of shell and star lights was to us a sight.
We dispersed off the buses at a place called Poperinghe,
And marched in deadly silence to a place called Vlamertinghe.
In the darkness wearily, we stumbled and plodded on,
To find some suitable resting place, to rest our limbs upon;
We were to have had shelter, in some huts that were found,
But luck was against us, we lay on open ground.
This night we will never forget, to our dying day,
In the cold and grizzly night, in the wet we lay;
But not for long, the order came for all to stand to.
The news went round like magic; the Huns were breaking through,
The news kindled up the flame that was rising in our veins,
To stop the Germans' gallop, we had to hold the reins;
It was now breaking daylight and awful sight were seen,
With hundreds of wounded soldiers returning from St. Jean.
Wes! Wounded were returning, all had the same old cry,
'Good luck to you, Durham lads, but you're going up to die'.
Our tired-out limbs were now forgot, we meant to make our name,
If we are going up there to die, we are going to die game;
Rain came down in torrents, and with shot and shell,
It was to us no other than a raging living hell.
We were now in the range of the enemy's guns,
Shells were dropping round us, I should say in tons,
At last the Hun's artillery had really found their mark,
And to be cut up by unseen foes, was to us no lark ...

Sergeant J. Wilkes

Spend Your Summer Holidays in Blighty. (*Plum & Apple*, October 1915, Tyne & Wear Archives)

The year would be remembered as one of deadlock. The French tried to break through in Artois and bled copiously. The British attacked and attacked again, finally and, most expensively, at Loos in September. Many lost their lives, and Sir John French was replaced by his former subordinate, Haig. The latter had milked every last ounce of influence and had zealously undermined his former chief. Everything in the trenches was in short supply, from shovels to hand grenades and, above all in 1915, artillery shells – the stuff of scandal.

Men, materials and money are the immediate necessities ... does the call of duty find no response in you until reinforced, let us say superseded, by the call of conscription?

What have you done?
What are you doing?
What are you going to do?
Will you help?
What can you do?

1. If a man of fighting age and fit – JOIN TODAY
2. If too old or working in munitions, or if a woman, get at least ONE RECRUIT TODAY!

Extract from Lord Kitchener's speech at the Guildhall,
9 July 1915

Edward Wyndham Tennant (1897–1916) was 17 in 1914. He was about to travel to Germany to improve his language skills before joining the Diplomatic Service. Instead, he enlisted with the Grenadier Guards. So efficient was he that the brigade rule which forbade officers under the age of 19 to be posted to France was ignored in his case and he became one of the youngest to serve. He was one month into his nineteenth year when he was shot by a sniper on the Somme.

LIGHT AFTER DARKNESS

ONCE more the Night, like some great dark drop-scene
Eclipsing horrors for a brief entr'acte,
Descends, lead-weighty. Now the space between,
Fringed with the eager eyes of men, is racked
By spark-tailed lights, curvetting far and high,
Swift smoke-flecked coursers, raking the black sky.

And as each sinks in ashes grey, one more
Rises to fall, and so through all the hours
They strive like petty empires by the score,
Each confident of its success and powers,
And, hovering at its zenith, each will show
Pale, rigid faces, lying dead, below.

There shall they lie, tainting the innocent air,
Until the dawn, deep veiled in mournful grey,
Sadly and quietly shall lay them bare,
The broken heralds of a doleful day.

E. Wyndham Tennant, Hulluch Road, October 1915

His last letter to his mother, Lady Glenconner, was written two days before his death:

To-night we go up to the trenches we were in, and to-morrow or the next day we go over the top … I am full of hope and trust, and I pray that I may be worthy of my fighting ancestors … I have never been prouder of anything, except your love for me, than I am of being a Grenadier.

In the line, in the vast labyrinth of trenches snaking across a scarred, lunar surface, enthusiasm and optimism had evaporated, sucked out by wounds and unending filth. Gains were bought at enormous cost, but could very often not be held. For all the killing opportunities offered by industrial war, there was still no form of tactical radio. The ability of the defender to slaughter attackers had passed the emphasis on to those holding ground rather than, as previously, those seeking to evict them.

*When this ****** war is over,*
Oh, how happy I shall be.
When I get my civvy clothes on,
No more soldiering for me.

Breaking this bitter stalemate proved impossible. Those survivors of the 'Old Contemptibles' who had made it through the winter now met their calvaries on Aubers Ridge, Festubert, Neuve Chapelle and Loos.

THE ROAD

There runs a road from Poperinghe,
Through Ypres to Zonnebeke, where winter, spring or summertime,
Are one unending trek.
For eastwards lies the enemy,
And westwards shines the sea,
And west to east, the men march on,
To keep their homeland free.

The maps all mark it yellow
And the lorries dust it white,
But it's black that road and bloody,
To the men that know it right,
For the trees are torn with shrapnel
And the pave's splashed with red
With gaping wounds by ditches side,
Where the guns have claimed the dead.

On runs the battered highway
Past broken walls and bare,
Through the city of all sorrows,
To the lone cathedral square,
But never a man that lingers,
Where the feet of kings have trod,
But on the steps with awe-struck eyes,
And a prayer in his heart to God.

And over the bridge of Menin,
And past the Menin Road,
Where the Red Cross vans come down from Hooge,
With their pitiful shattered load.
On to the Polzje crossroads,
Or northward to St. Jean,

And heaven help your transport,
If the big guns catch it then.

But, this side of Verlorenhoek,
The marching feet stop still,
For a thin brown breastwork holds them,
At the gates of a water-mill,
But the desolate road runs onward,
Barren and overgrown,
Where death, the wanton, beckoning, reckoning,
Walks in the night alone.

What of the men who trod it,
Who will tread no road again,
The wind in the nodding poplars,
Whispers their message plain.
Still eastwards lies the enemy,
And westwards shines the sea,
March from west to east, march on,
To keep our homeland free.

Lieutenant Hugh Lyon, 6th Durham Light Infantry

Things Nurses must not do.

1. Nurses must not be late on duty.
2. Nurses must not wear blogs.
3. Nurses must not touch the "Goods".
4. Nurses must not dab their hands on "Troops" early in the morning.
5. Nurses must not chatter in the wards after "Lights Out".
6. Nurses must not carry Fore-ceps with which to torment the wounds of the "Troops".
7. Nurses must not carry on "Flirtations" with the "Troops".
8. Nurses must not on any account kiss the "Troops".
9. Nurses must not forget water for the Troops to wash their Teeth in.
10. Nurses must not allow their eyes to wander during the rising of the "Troops".
11. Nurses must not forget to give "Scullery Boy" tea when taking some themselves.

P.T.O.

Things Nurses must not do. (Drawing in autograph book, 1914–18, author's own)

Despite this murderous baptism, many Territorials ('Saturday night soldiers') still managed to churn the horror into verse.

We've served with you for near a year
And shared your woes and joys
We shall miss your lengthy shadow
And so will all the boys
But when we're digging trenches, Jim
We shall always think of you.
Instead of digging four feet six,
We'll dig them six foot two!

Plum & Apple, October 1915

Charles Scott-Moncrieff (1889–1930) was a writer and transla-
tor who joined the Kings Own Scottish Borderers in 1914. He
was invalided out of the Army after the Battle of Arras in 1917
and was to limp for the rest of his life as a result of his injury.
The title of this poem comes from the school song at Winchester,
which Scott-Moncrieff attended. It refers to an idealised, nostalgic
view of English public schools, as well as a celebration of the end
of term and impending freedom. It is understood to refer to the
Battle for Hill 60.

DOMUM (OMNIBUS WICCAMICIS)

*The green and grey and purple day is barred with clouds
of dun,
From Ypres city smouldering before the setting sun;
Another hour will see it flower, lamentable sight,
A bush of burning roses underneath the night.*

*Who's to fight for Flanders, who will set them free,
The war-worn lowlands by the English sea?
Who, my young companions, will choose a way to war,
That Marlborough, Wellington, have trodden out before?*

*Are these mere names? Then hear a solemn sound:
The blood of our brothers is crying from the ground:
'What we dared and died for, what the rest may do,
Little sons of Wykeham, is it naught to you?'*

*'Father and Founder, our feet may never more
Tread the stones of Flint-Court or Gunner's green shore,
But wherever they assemble, we are pressing near,
Calling and calling: could our brothers hear!'*

What was it you fought for, whose profit that you died?
Here is Ypres burning and twenty towns beside,
Where is the gain in all our pain when he we loved but
now
Is lying still on Sixty Hill, a bullet through his brow?

'He died one thing regarding that is better worth
Than the golden cities of all the kings on earth.
Were right and wrong to choose among, he had seen the
right,
Had found the thing appointed and done it with his might.'

'Thus I muse, regarding, with a pensive eye,
Towered Ypres blazing, beneath the night sky ...
This way may lie failure, but Towers there are that stand,
Hence, it may be, guarded, in our own green land.'

Charles Scott-Moncrieff, St Eloi, June 1915

On 20 November 1915, 2nd Lieutenant Gamble of the Durhams acquainted his readers with a new parody of 'Little Grey Home in the West':

> There's a shallow wet trench near Houplines
> 'Tis the wettest there ever has been,
> There are bullets that fly,
> There are shells in the sky,
> And it smells like a German 'has been'.
>
> My dug-out's a haven of rest,
> Though it's only a tumble down nest,
> But with 'Johnsons' around,
> I must keep underground,
> Till the golden sun sinks in the west.

The war took on new dimensions of horror when, at Second Ypres, the Germans first deployed chlorine gas: a creeping yellow cloud of blind malevolence. Canadian soldiers, with no gas masks, were told to urinate on their handkerchiefs and then tie these around their faces, the ammonia offering some protection. They fought on. Despite the terrible realities of this most modern of wars, such luminaries as Sir Arthur Conan Doyle could still bang out patriotic homilies:

AN EXTRACT FROM *YPRES*

Push on, my Lord of Wurttemberg, push on, across the fen!
See where the lure of Ypres calls you!
There's just one ragged British line of Plumer's weary men,
It's true they held you off before, but venture it again!
Come, try your luck, whatever fate befalls you!

You've been some little time, my Lord. Perhaps you scarce remember
The far-off days of that resistance.
Was it in October last? Or was it in November?
And now the leaves are turning and you stand in mid-September
Still staring at the Belfry in the distance.

Can you recall the fateful day – a day of drifting skies,
When you started on the famous Calais onset?
Can it be the Warlord blundered when he urged the enterprise?
For surely it's a weary while since first before your eyes
The old Belfry rose against the sunset.

You held council at your quarters, when the budding Alexanders,
And the Pickel-haubed Caesars gave their reasons.
Was there one amongst that bristle-headed circle of commanders,
Ever ventured the opinion that a little town of Flanders
Would hold you pounded here through all the seasons!

You all clasped hands upon it. You would break the British line,
You would smash a road to westward with your host,
The howitzers would thunder and the Uhlan lances shine,
Till Calais heard the blaring of the distant 'Wacht am Rhein',
As you topped the grassy uplands of the coast.

And so next day your battle rolled across the Menin Plain,
Where Capper's men stood lonely to your wrath,
You broke him, and you broke him, but you broke him all in vain,
For he and his Contemptibles kept closing up again,
And the khaki bar was still across your path.

And on the day when Gheluvelt lay smoking in the sun,
When von Deimling stormed so hotly in the van,
You smiled as Haig reeled backwards and you thought him on the run,
But alas for dreams that vanish, for before the day was done,
It was you, my Lord of Wurttemberg that ran.

A dreary day was that – but another came, more dreary,
When the Guard from Arras led your fierce attacks,
Spruce and splendid in the morning were the Potsdam Grenadiers,
But not so spruce that evening when they staggered spent and weary,
With those cursed British storming at their backs.

You knew – your spies had told you – that the ranks were scant and thin,
That the guns were short of shell and very few,
By all Bernhard's maxims you were surely bound to win,
There's the town open before you. Haste, my Lord and enter in,
Or the Warlord may have telegrams for you.

Then came the rainy winter, when the price was ever dearer,
Every time you neared the prize of which you dreamed,
Each day the Belfry faced you, but you never brought it nearer,
Each night you saw it clearly, but you never saw it clearer.
Ah, what a weary time it must have seemed!

At last there came the Easter when you loosed the coward gases,
Surely you have got the rascals now!
You could see them spent and choking as you watched them through
your glasses,
Yes, they choke, but never waver, and again the moment passes,
Without one laurel for your brow.

Sir Arthur Conan Doyle

Those at the 'sharp end' saw things rather differently in that year:

THE THINGS THAT MATTER

'Twas in the war, nineteen fifteen, at early dawn one day.
Our orders were to take the trench which opposite us lay.
The battle raged around us fierce, the air was thick with shell,
But no man flinched as we advanced to drive the Hun to hell.

Our object gained, we paused awhile to get our breath much needed
(And all this time, I'd have you know, the battle still proceeded)
The ground behind us now was swept by all the hostile guns,
To stop reserves from coming up – a habit of the Huns.

On glancing back, to my surprise I suddenly observed
From out the smoke a figure rush, a VC he deserved;
'Go back,' I cried, 'Go back at once' – my words passed quite unheeded
(And all this time, as I've remarked, the battle still proceeded).

He reached our trench though wounded thrice and, as he fainted,
A message form into my hand, that gallant soldier planted.
'What's this?' I gasped, as I read out the message written there,
'Report at once the method used by you to cut men's hair'.

'No time to lose,' I shouted out; 'now who will volunteer
To take the answer back "at once", though 'twill be late I fear?'
'Let me go, sir' the cry went up from every lusty throat.
I picked a man, then sat me down, and this reply I wrote.

The method used by me to cut the hair of men who need it
Is sometimes just to burn it off, and other times to weed it
And often rasps are used instead; these latter cause some bleeding
(I'd like to add, to let you know, the battle's still proceeding).

With bated breath we watched him start, the gallant man selected
To take the message back to those by whom it was expected.
'Twas with relief we saw him gain a spot from whence we knew
He could proceed with safety with his message to HQ.

'The war is won,' I told my men. 'No need to use our rifles
While those behind look after us, we need not think of trifles,
Such as the Hun in front of us or when it's time for feeding'
(But all the same, I'm loath to say, the battle's still proceeding!)

Anon.

The name of Ypres would now and forever be etched into our consciousness.

ILIUM

Fair was your city, old and fair
And fair the hall where the kings abode,
And you speak to us in your despair,
To us who see but ruins bare,
A crumbled wall, a shattered stair,
And graves on the Menin Road.

It was sweet you say, from the city wall,
To watch the fields where the horsemen rode,
It was sweet to hear at even fall,
Across the moat, the voices call.
It was good to see the stately hall,
From the paths by the Menin Road.

Yea, citizens of the city dead,
Whose souls are torn by memories goad,
But now there are stones in the Cloth Hall's stead,
And the moat that you loved is sometimes red,
And vices are still and laughter sped.
And torn is the Menin Road.

And by the farms and the House of White,
And the shrine where the little candle glowed,
There is silence now by day and night,
Or the sudden crash and the blinding light,
For the guns smite ever as thunders smite,
And there's death on the Menin Road.

Anon.

1916: DEATH

It would all change in 1916. Haig and Joffre, the French commander-in-chief, had agreed upon a joint offensive. Their German counterpart, Von Falkenhayn, pre-empted this by a mighty onslaught against the French bastion of Verdun. He wasn't seeking breakthrough, just grinding attrition to strain French resources to breaking point.

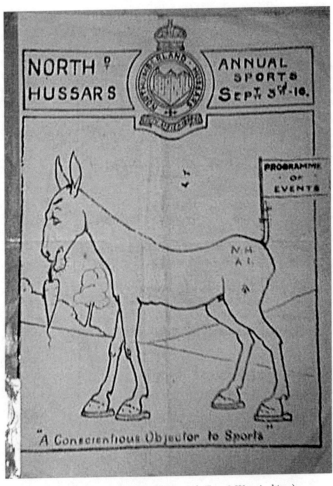

A Conscientious Objector to Sports. (Plum & *Apple*, Tyne & Wear Archives)

PUZZLED

With occasional eatin' and drinkin'
An' just forty winks now and then
An' work on the trenches
Along o' the Frenchies
We don't get much time for thinking,
We men!

An' what me an' my company ain't yet made out,
Is wot's this 'ere culture they're talkin' about?
Though we don't get no 'Specials' we've had a
Round dozen who tell the same tale
How Germans will pillage
A poor little village
And quiet the natives by murder
Wholesale.

An' what me an' my company ain't yet made out,
Is wot's this 'ere culture they're talkin' about?
They slash up the pictures with sabres,
Which seems a bit spiteful an' odd,
Wi' search lights they shows up,
The churches they blows up
An' [Kaiser] Bill when they've ended their labours,
Thanks God!

An' what me an' my company ain't yet made out,
Is wot's this 'ere culture they're talkin' about?
Then the brave kindly men will strip lasses
An' mothers and wives to their skin
And when they're a-cryin'
An' hopin' they're dyin'
Will jeer at each one as she passes
An' grin!

An' what me an' my company ain't yet made out,
Is wot's this 'ere culture they're talkin' about?
I'm reckoned an 'ot argumenter
An' fust-rate at waggin' me chin
But sharp as a bay'nit
I can't explain it
An' shan't till we've licked 'em an' enter Berlin.

An' what me an' my company ain't yet made out,
Is wot's this 'ere culture they're talkin' about?

Anon.

Those who have heard anything about the Great War will probably have heard of the Somme. As with Verdun for the French, it symbolises the loss of a generation, a frightful gobbling up of blood and manhood for trifling gains.

Beef steaks when you are hungry,
Best beer when you are dry,
Fivers when you are hard up,
Heaven when you die!

Private M. Gill, 8th Battalion Leicesters

Along the otherwise insignificant ridge running from Thiepval to Ginchy, the Germans had turned sleepy hamlets into bristling fortresses. General Rawlinson, commanding the Fourth Army, was an advocate of 'bite and hold': a series of limited assaults, each quickly consolidated and then built up in readiness for the next. Haig needed rather more, he had to have breakthrough. His political masters demanded no less.

> *On 1st July 1916, the first day of the battle of the Somme, many thousands of Englishmen, mostly young Englishmen – were killed. That was a day of terrible, heavy casualties and it was our first experience on a great scale of the bloodiness of modern war. Two thousand men were killed trying to cross a piece of ground not as big as Orchard Field; trying, for they failed. It is no use trying to describe the conditions during a great attack for, since my own experience of them, I have always been convinced that no-one who had not been there could possibly even imagine the effect on body and mind of all that is heard and seen and felt by those who are taking part.*

Sermon by Stanley Purvis MA, November 1943

The British would attack at zero hour (7.30 a.m.) on 1 July.

THE TYNESIDE SCOTTISH AT THE BATTLE OF THE SOMME

Now listen to my story
I won't keep you long
It's about the Tyneside Scottish
And the Battle of the Somme

It was on July the First
When the Scottish made to attack
The shells began to burst
But that didn't keep them back

Oh, it was a terrible day,
They fought with all their might
Poor fellows, they were falling
Both on the left and right

And when all was over
I am sorry to relate
All that we could number was
One hundred and twenty-eight

Now my friends, remember
What the local lads have done –
They fought and died for their country's sake,
At the Battle of the Somme

Private M. Woodhouse, 1st Battalion Tyneside Scottish

Casualty lists mounted steadily. The British crept forward, not in bounds but in blood-garnished yards. Still no sign of breakthrough.

There are several sorts of peaches,
But I find in you alone
The one that's full; of sweetness
And without a heart of stone.

Private W.G. Glenn (wounded near Thiepval on 8 May 1916), 9th Battalion Royal Inniskilling Fusiliers

On taking over a billet in October, Charles Moss and the Durham Pals found this helpful ode written on the wall:

Harken all ye whom duty calls
To spend some time within these friendly walls,
Others will sojourn here when you have passed,
You were not the first and will not be the last,
Therefore take heed and do what ye may,
For safety or comfort while ye stay!
Just put a sandbag here, a picture there
To make a room more safe, a wall less bare,
Think as you tread the thorny path of duty,
Of comfort, of security, and beauty,
So your successors when they come shall say
'A fine battalion we relieved today'.

The battle dragged on through the summer and into the autumn, with final gasps during November.

FROM ONE WHO KNOWS

There's many a private soldier,
Who walks his humble way
With no sounding name or title
Unknown to the world today,
In the eyes of God is a hero
As worthy of the days
As any mighty general,
To whom the world gives praise.

Private C. Wiles, 20th Battalion Middlesex Regiment

UNOFFICIAL ORDERS

From Colonel MacEmfit, commanding the Umpteenth (Reserve) Battalion, County of London Regiment (the London Skittish):

1. Parades – tomorrow being the day after tonight, there will, of course, be no parades.

2. Medical – men who wake up during the night suffering from 'Haggis Fever' are warned against dipping their heads in the fire bucket as the contact with cold water is extremely apt to bring on the dreaded 'Tartan Rush' which would, in all probability, necessitate the immediate transfer of the sufferer to some other highland regiment as his face would, of course, clash with the hodden grey!

3. Plank beds – men are warned that they should be careful to see that the three planks making up the bed all bend evenly when lain upon, otherwise men may get nipped in the bud!

London Scottish Regimental Gazette, December 1916

Yorkshireman's motto. (Drawing in autograph book, 1914–18, author's own)

One who went through the Somme grinder was A.P. Herbert, the noted humorist, playwright, writer and law reform activist, perhaps best known for his *Misleading Cases*. He served in the Royal Naval Division (RND), an anachronistic unit which was very much Navy yet fought on land. Being Navy, the battalions had their own jealously guarded traditions which clashed with military practice. General Shute, a Regular Army martinet, was not well liked:

THE GENERAL INSPECTING THE TRENCHES

The General inspecting the trenches
exclaimed with a horrified shout,
'I refuse to command a Division
Which leaves its excreta about.'

And certain responsible critics
Made haste to reply to his words
Observing that his Staff advisers
Consisted entirely of turds.

But nobody took any notice
No one was prepared to refute,
That the presence of shit was congenial
Compared with the presence of Shute.

For shit may be shot at odd corners
And paper supplied there to suit,
But a shit would be shot without mourners
If somebody shot that shit Shute.

A.P. Herbert

THE MOST WORSHIPFUL COMPANY OF NARQUES PRESENT – AN AGREEABLE COMEDY OF MANNERS, ENTITLED 'THE SOLDIER'S BRIDE'

Furnishings by Torqueraca et Cie
Wiggins by C.O. Peppery
Lights by the 'Maison Chef'
Accidental music by Private H. Arnold Smith

NOTICE: The attention of the audience is respectfully drawn to Section 3 of Chapter 101, Xi, Qeo III entitled 'An Act to prohibit the infliction of bodily harm on Mummers or other Common Persons':

'It shall be a misdemeanour for anyone to fling at or towards any person giving or attempting to give a theatrical representation, any coins, oranges, bags containing confectionery, or other dangerous substances, with the object of inflicting bodily harm upon the aforesaid Mummer or Mimic unless it shall sufficiently appear that such throwing as aforesaid and the immediate obliteration of the hereinbefore mentioned Mummer or Mimic is urgently necessary in the interests of the Public safety.'

For the Lord Chamberlain at Buckingham Palace, this 7th Day of December, 1916

For every jocular line penned by the wags, there were more like this:

Dear Madam,

I regret to have to break this sad news to you regarding your husband, whom I'm sorry to tell you was shot through the head this morning by a sniper; he was unconscious until he died. It has been a sad blow to me and all his chums for he was well respected by all with whom he came into contact with. We did the best we could for him when we saw there was no hope of recovery. His platoon sergeant and chums knelt and said the Rosary and De Profundas and a few acts of contrition as we were Roman Catholics like himself. He died the death of a hero, he was a soldier and a man. Please accept the sympathy of myself and all his comrades. Gone but not forgotten.

Yours truly, 12685 Sergeant Brammer and 9725 Sergeant Halpin

Private M. O'Donnell, 14th Battalion Durham Light Infantry, was killed on 26 February 1916. He was a shipyard worker and had been with Short's for fifteen years prior to enlisting.

Arthur Lewis Jenkins (1892–1917) had hoped to join the Indian Civil Service and served there for a year before transferring to Aden. He learned to fly in Egypt, returning to England to join a home defence squadron of the Royal Flying Corps.

OUTPOSTS

WHEN the moonlit shadows creep,
When the sun beats pitiless down,
Steadfast, vigilant they keep
Watch and ward about the town.

Guardians of an Empire's gate,
In the sunshine and the dust
Still beside their guns they wait,
Faithful to their weary trust.

Not for them the hero's cross,
Not for them the hero's grave,
Thrill of victory, pain of loss,
Praise of those they fell to save.

Only days of monotone,
Sand and fever, flies and fret,
All unheeded and unknown,
Little thanks they're like to get.

Yet mayhap in after-days
Distant eye the clearer sees
Gods apportioning the praise
Shall be kindly unto these.

A.L. Jenkins

Arthur Jenkins was killed in a plane crash on New Year's Eve 1917.

All that glorious enthusiasm seemed a long way off. A generation had come of age with a terrible rite of passage. Kenneth Herbert Ashley (1887–?) was an English poet, novelist, journalist and farmer. He had a deep love of the English countryside and rural life; a passion reflected in *Up Hill and Down Dale* (1923), his experience forever marked by the war.

CLOSE OF PLAY

I wonder if Life is kind or callous
When it fails to warn us of final things —
When we make an End: and no revelation
Informs the heart with forebodings?

I remember a hazy day in August:
A hazy day with a smudge of sun:
When a score of fellows played at cricket —
Twenty and two, and I was one.
Harry, I know, was playing against me;
Fast off break, and he'd found a spot:
I flicked at one, and was caught at the wicket
The umpire said; but I thought not.
And I remember in the pavilion
I sat and talked the usual rot;
Then caught a train, and what happened else on
That casual day I have forgot.
But O' how different a meaning
The day would have held if I had known!
I would have stayed to see the finish,
The last run made and the last ball thrown;
And when the umpires came slowly walking,
And the wickets no longer stood intact,
I would have made an end of talking,
Feeling the ritual of the act.

A wee hot Scotch. (Author's own)

And Harry and I, as it befitted,
Would have waited to stand beside the ring,
Where only the swallows dived and twittered,
To hear the beat of another wing.
And we would have sat all night together,
Till nothing was left unsaid.
And we would have turned to greet the dawning,
Knowing our youth was dead.
But of these things we had no warning,
Never a hint at all:
That Harry had bowled his final over,
That I had finished with bat and ball.

Kenneth H. Ashley

Surrender! British Cavalry Beat and Cow the Hun. (*War Illustrated*, 28 April 1917, p.245)

1917: MUD

For Sir Douglas Haig, 1917 would not be a vintage year. His opening offensives at Arras and Vimy achieved wonders at the outset, though the former swiftly degenerated into costly attrition. General Plumer and the Second Army performed tremendous feats at Messines, but then Haig's great summer offensive, the Third Battle of Ypres, popularly known by the name of one of its objectives, Passchendaele, became the very symbol of fruitless slaughter in a hellish sea of mud.

For old hands like Charles Moss, any gloss of patriotism had long since worn off:

KITCHENER'S ARMY SOLDIERS CHRISTMAS DAY
IN THE WORKHOUSE

'Tis Christmas day in the workhouse,
The paupers are called up in their groups,
The only men left here to grouse
Are the broken or lead-swinging troops

You ask me why the troops grouse sir,
When they've still got three limbs and an eye,
It's not that they're broken in body sir,
They're broken in pocket that's why

Don't think they're fed up with the workhouse,
'Cause they're fed the best of them all,
Far better than most of the mob sir,
Who've not answered their country's call

Of all the war billets they've had sir,
Like shell-fired farms out in France,
To sleep on a clean wooden floor sir
This Christmas, they're glad of the chance

You ask if there's any complaints sir
It's not just the rations you mean?
A soldier should never complain sir
But I'll tell you what I have seen

Our sergeant's a sarcastic time server,
Done his soldiering on the barrack square
And a bit on that big fatigue sir,
They call the South African War

He's never been 'up the line' sir
Or ever been 'over the lid'

Nor seen the square-headed swine sir
Behind a bombing-post hid

He don't understand Kitchener's Mob sir
Thinks soldiering is just dressing up,
Saluting and drawing your bob [n] sir,
And getting plenty of beer to sup

He sang, 'Oh, What a Lovely War' sir
While we 'stood-to' in the trenches,
He went 'square-pushing' all trim sir
Then in the sex-war with the wenches

These BEF boys in the workhouse
Don't need 'spit and polish' parades
They're more used to going at night sir
On patrols and Mills-bombing raids!

Charles Moss

The sheer weight of slaughter, the vast, unending casualty lists and general war weariness had not completely eliminated the gloss of sentiment:

HEROES OF HOME

The boy has gone with his heart aglow
In an alien land to fight,
The mother who bore him watched him go,
And her trembling lips were white,
Yet she had bidden him strike his blow,
For his King and the cause of Right!

The boy in the midst of toil and fight
Small time can spare for thought,
The mother who sent him dreams all night
Of battles he never fought,
And seems him wounded, in desperate plight
Or by brutal captors caught!

He takes his hardship as so much sport
Being far too busy to whine,
But anxious fears at home distort
Each peril into time
The crowded hour is always short;
'Tis waiting hearts that pine!

He fell at last with thousands more –
Just one of thousands slain –
On a day when the land was drenched with gore,
From Dixmuide to the Aisne,
And he lay in peace in a world at war
And knew not toil nor pain.

The mother who sent him bowed her head
And wept for the lad she bore
Yet never she grudged her sacred dead
For her country's need was sore
'He died for his King and the Right', she said
'And no man could do more'.

But the dead, proud heart of her inly bled,
Though she showed her grief to none;
She was just one woman who mourned her dead
Out of many thousands – one!
But it's better to die when the blood runs red
Than to live when hope is done.

Eric Fitzwalter Wilkinson

The commander-in-chief's woes multiplied when compliant Asquith was replaced by fiery Lloyd George as Prime Minister. Both general and politician detested each other. The Welshman was understandably appalled by the losses incurred on the Somme and described Haig as 'a military Moloch'.

Lieutenant Arthur Terry, destined to see hard service at Arras, served as quartermaster to the 4th Battalion Tyneside Scottish, 23rd Northumberland Fusiliers. He was a constant and detailed correspondent to his wife Dora, to whom he wrote on 2 January 1917:

Don't faint! I'm enclosing my promised poem; I'll bet you 8d [4p] you can't beat it. It isn't quite up to the highest standard but then it's wartime you know!

Oh, thou who art the mainspring of my life
My dearest love, my very dearest wife
(That sounds as though of wives I had a few
But truly I have none excepting you)
Pray read between the lines of my poor lay
All that my feeble pen can never say
(By rhyming all these lines, I think there's six
I've mastered one at least of poet's tricks)
I long once more, oh how I long my Dora
To feel the spell of thy benign aura
(I rather pride myself on these two rhymes
The poet in me comes out strong at times)
I long to see they face – to hear thy voice
I'd fly to there at once had I the choice
(You'll notice that in couplets I must write
I fear that otherwise I would take all night)
I think of those at home while here I stay
And sadly muse the long, long hours away
(That's the Dickensian, sentimental touch;
I hope it will be regarded as such)

The night is cold and damp – it rains and rains
Indoors I woo my muse until my brains
Racked and tormented, swear they'll go no farther
So I'll conclude, your loving husband, Arthur.

That same week, Lieutenant Terry extended his creative repertoire by taking to the boards on 4 January 1917:

I've made my first appearance in panto and as I didn't get hissed off the stage or have rotten eggs thrown at me, I suppose I didn't hurt the show!

Brisk Business Behind the British Lines. (*War Illustrated*, 31 March 1917, p.139)

Charles Moss, holding no great respect for rank and title and not one to tolerate fools, had a genuine love for his comrades, regardless of their backgrounds:

PRIVATE TOMMY ATKINS

On army forms 'Tommy's' the name he bears
But in the ranks this Monica's no good
If he's a Murphy, whatever he cares
He'll get no other name than 'Spud'.
And if he's one of the family Clark
And was baptised Fred, or Jack, or Bobby
Or uses his number to keep it dark,
He will always loudly be called 'Nobby'.

And if his true surname should be Miller
Let him be a fraud, or good and trusty,
A man or a mouse or a ladykiller,
You'll find he will always be called 'Dusty'!

Soldiers must ever be ready to die
When they get their baptism of fire,
And be forgotten, wherever they lie,
But their nicknames will never expire.

Charles Moss

George Purvis was the son of Major J.B. Purvis of Bridlington. Both father and son practised as pharmacists and opticians. George was educated at the local Grammar School where he was active in the Officer Training Corps (OTC) and mentored the shooting team. From OTC colour-sergeant, he progressed to 2nd lieutenant in the Territorials (5th Battalion Green Howards). He went to France in April 1915 and first saw action at Second Ypres. Latterly, he was promoted to command a machine-gun company and was Mentioned in Dispatches on 9 April 1916. Both his father and younger brother, Stanley, also served. The boys' mother wrote of her husband and sons:

... these are all my men, and I am proud to feel they all held commissions before the outbreak of the war.

Officers' diaries reflect the endless stream of routine chores and the considerable burden of responsibility which they carried. Junior officers, from subaltern to lieutenant, carried a heavier load as they remained responsible for the daily needs of their platoon and day to day maintenance and digging of trenches. As battalions were routinely moved from sector to sector, the grind was continuous. The higher up the command chain an officer advanced, the further he was distanced from the day to day and the greater his power to delegate. Generally, his prospects for survival increased. Attrition was worst at junior level with six weeks being the average life expectancy of an infantry subaltern. The odds were rather more stacked against him than the non-commissioned officers (NCOs) and men under his command. On 17 May 1915, George Purvis wrote to his brother:

My Dear Kid,

Many thanks for your letter received about ten days ago. I hardly know where to begin and what to tell you, I have seen and done as many different things. Of course you being an officer can have things told you which could not be sent to the ordinary civilian, a sort of private notes from the Front. If I do this it puts you in rather an awkward position as then you become the censor of your own letters and must decide what shall be passed on for general information. I will try and take a between course. As you will see by the appearance of this letter it is raining and I am writing this in a very leaky hut in 'Rest' (pleasant) Camp.

I may say that the gales are produced by holes in the roof and walls. These holes were made by shrapnel bullets and fragments of shell on one of the periodic bombardments the camp is subjected to, within about a foot of my head as I sleep is a fair sized hole where a shell has exploded having come through the wall first.

Last night as I was out with a fatigue party we had the pleasure of seeing our happy little home shelled and found that the battalion had had to take to their dug outs for about an hour. Also early this morning when we were first getting up they gave us quite a nice little firework display, plumping between 30–40 Jack Johnsons [heavy artillery shells] into the camp in salvoes of 3 at a time. No one was hit, although many of the men got quite useful mementoes which fell near them!

Since writing to you we have been tramping about France and Belgium moving almost every night. Sleeping in all sorts of weird places, resting during the day mostly as it is too hot to march then except in cases of great necessity and then we are rushed up by motor buses. Practically everything has to be done at night as the German aeroplanes [sic] are so active during the day. It is quite a common thing to see 8 or 9 aeroplanes of various nationalities up at once 50% of which are being fired at either by our anti aircraft guns or those of the Germans.

I will give you just a few of the places I have slept in since leaving England. First of all one night in a ship's bunk, next night in a tent on a very cold night in H–, next night in a French First Class Carriage, the next were in cattle trucks 40–45 in each then for seven nights in a nice clean cowshed full of straw. After this we went into the trenches I inhabited my farm No 77 St–. We returned to wooden huts which were shelled while we were in them and had to occupy our dug outs which we had made during the day. Next night we trekked further back about 7 miles and bivouacked in a grass field with only the stars above. Moved again next night and spent the day riding back to the huts to bring up some stores which had been left behind. It rained slightly most of this day. The second night we billeted in a little village of A–. My rest in a sort of jack of all trades establishment composed of 1, a shop, 2, Gendarmerie, 3, a Grocers shop, 4, a tobacco factory and cigarette store, 5, a farm and mill on a small scale.

I myself found a lodging in a second rate estaminet in a very small, short continental bed. It is their shortness which I dislike most in these continental beds. Move again that night. I spent most of the day sleeping in beautiful grass fields, move again that evening arriving in good billets about 9 am. We stayed in this place for about five days.

1. Remembered Faces. (Drawing in autograph book, 1914–18, author's own)

2. An optimist. (Authors' collection)

LEISURE.

What is this life if, full of care,
We have no time to stand and stare?
No time to stand beneath the boughs
And stare as long as sheep or cows.
No time to see, when woods we pass,
Where squirrels hide their nuts in grass.
No time to turn at Beauty's glance,
And watch her feet, how they can dance.
A poor life this if, full of care,
We have no time to stand and stare.

3. Leisure. (Authors' collection)

4. Plum & Apple –
Northumberland Hussars
Newsletter. (October 1915,
Tyne & Wear Archives)

5. Her Majesty the Queen. (*The Queen's Gift Book: In aid of Queen Mary's Convalescent Auxiliary Hospitals – For Soldiers and Sailors who have lost their limbs in the war* (Hodder and Stoughton, 1915). Authors' collection)

PEOPLE we have "STRAFFED"
THE ORDERLY OFFICER
In two straaf's

When at stables you're kept slaving
And the day is fussed hot
The horses are ill-tempered
And the Sergeants swear a lot
Don't curse the British Army
Or sing the 'Hymn of Hate'
Just strafe the Orderly Officer
For keeping you so late

When you hasten to the 'Staminet
With a fierce and raging thirst
To find that it is 'ferme
The M.P's been there first
Don't lose your temper Trooper
Or, with Madam be irate
Just strafe the Orderly Officer
For keeping you so late.

MISFORTUNES during th MONTH

Drummond Lieut. H---- ---- .... A.D.C. to H.Q's
Noonan Pte. E. .... Wounded
Burn " N .... "
Hansen Far Sgt .... MARRIED
Lee Pte. R .... Wounded
Boothroyd . R.E .... Ret'd to duty
A Mule .... Taken on to strength
Draft .... Arrived

7. Memories of Home – Tanfield. (Drawing in autograph book, 1914–18, author's own)

8. His Majesty the King. (*The Queen's Gift Book* (Hodder and Stoughton, 1915). Authors' collection)

9. Cheeky Chappie. (Drawing in autograph book, 1914–18, author's own)

10. Ward 25 – June 1918. (Drawing in autograph book, 1914–18, author's own)

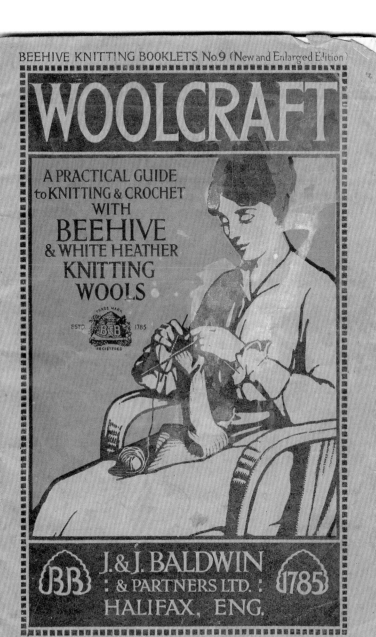

WOOLCRAFT

A PRACTICAL GUIDE
to KNITTING & CROCHET
WITH
BEEHIVE
& WHITE HEATHER
KNITTING
WOOLS

TRADE MARK
ESTD. BB 1785
REGISTERED

J. & J. BALDWIN
: & PARTNERS LTD. :
HALIFAX, ENG.

BB   1785

1. Comforts from home – knitting for the boys. (Author's own)

12. The Quality of Mercy. (*The Queen's Gift Book* (Hodder and Stoughton, 1915). Authors' collection)

The first day we were here Gen French spoke very complimentary and encouraging words to us making us very proud to be Territorials and practically saying that we had saved the situation.

Certainly, all seemed very touch and go at the time but the situation has improved immensely in the last three weeks. We ought to be very proud as it is no doubt a distinction us being sent straight into the thickest of the heavy fighting round there when there are Territorial battalions who have been in France since November of last year and have got nowhere near the firing line and only just got within hearing of the guns about 10 days after we had come from the trenches. After our five days in S— we were once more taken up towards the A line in buses. We however only occupied some trenches and dug outs well in rear but still well within the danger zone from their artillery. Those two nights I slept under a wagon, a very warm place for a 'bivvy' too I can tell you. The third night we moved still nearer the 7 line and occupied more dug outs but the men had to dig themselves in as there were not sufficient room for them.

I might as well tell you now that we dig ourselves in every time we halt for more than a few minutes and then I need not tell you that 'every night we dug ourselves in'. It is a standing order so I will not repeat it every time. These nights we sent out digging parties who went to various parts of the line and helped R.E [Royal Engineers] to build new trenches, carry for them and generally make themselves useful. The rule is generally that the party works till 1 am and then gets back to its billet where they generally arrive between 2.30 or 3.30 am according to the distance.

It is rather risky work because you are generally working only about 1000 yards from the front trenches and the Germans send up their star shells all night and desultory rifle and artillery fire just to keep things lively. We stayed in our dug outs 2 days and then some artillery came in and mounted their guns near us and made things too likely to be uncomfortable and dangerous so we moved still nearer the firing line and came to our old rest camp where the Germans have been giving us presents and souvenirs in the shape of shot and shells at intervals when they think we shall be 'at home'.

An extract from a Tommy's letter: 'I think we have them whacked, what I said that time, they have as much chance as a snowball in Hell!' A very good simile I think. Censoring letters is an awful business and wastes an awful lot of time if you do it properly. I must say the men are mostly very good and keep off prohibited subjects very well. It is the men who get home sick and wounded who talk about things which they should not and of course they cannot be stopped. They spin some awful yarns which get into the papers. For instance, one of my men who'd had colic and was sent to hospital wrote home to tell them he had been 'gassed'.

As a matter of fact, he was left behind in our farm No 77 when the section went forward to the battalion as he had been sent up in daylight and had been sniped and it had got on his nerves. On the way back we were shelled with these beastly gas shells and there is no doubt it is beastly stuff. I got quite enough for my liking. It makes you eyes smart so that you cannot see and breathing also is made very difficult but the shells are nothing half so bad as those they send out of tubes from cylinders under pressure. Fortunately, our battalion never got dosed with that but I believe the 4th Battalion did, much to their discomfort.

I will now tell you a little about one of the most interesting Sundays I have ever spent. I think we had a very good church parade in the morning, spent the rest of the day in writing and censoring letters, watching the aeroplanes [sic] skimming about the sky and being shelled if they got too far over each other's lines. Then at 5.30 pm we paraded 200 men for digging. We marched 2 miles back to draw tools and then advanced about 5 miles forward to our 'digging'.

I had often wanted to go to the same town as Earp, got the stained glass from the Cathedral, in daylight but could never get permission. However, my journey this time caused me to cross right through the centre of it. It was an object lesson in the power of the modern explosive. The Germans have been shelling this place since October with every kind of gun and shell that they have got from 17" Howitzers to 4th grade firers. The whole place is a desolation, streets gutted by fire, others simply heaps of broken bricks.

The famous buildings simply a few isolated features such as a wall with two pinnacles on top connected by a very tumbledown wall to a tower and the other end that was the Cathedral. The other famous place was in a little better repair and it retained a glorious grandeur even in its desolation.

To come to more mundane things, the streets were littered with stinking carcase of dead horses, broken wagons and carts of furniture, shell holes of all sizes, but always circular and a general air of desolation and putrescence. I saw one shell hole where it was 42 feet across and over 20 feet deep. At the bottom was a dead horse! One small grass field outside the town would not be an acre in area, had at least a dozen large shell holes in it. It looked more like the holey end of a bagatelle board. We saw a high class hotel which had simply been left as it stood in ordinary everyday life, windows and doors were smashed but clean glasses and bottles full of various wines stood on the shelves. Tables and chairs were set out and even though except for the effects of the bombardment, it was as before.

When we got to our trench which we had to improvise and strengthen the parapet a lively night attack was taking place and the bullets were whistling and thudding down unnecessarily close. We also got presents of shells, 50% of which did not explode. The battlefield on a nice starlight night attack is most picturesque with star-lights going up all around and flashes from the guns and bursting shells and the general din. It was all very fierce.

Must close; with much love your affectionate brother, George.

George Purvis was killed on 8 June 1917. At the time of his death, George had orders to return to England to take up a post as an instructor at a machine-gun training school. He delayed his departure from the line because his company was very short of trained and experienced officers.

Belgian Slaves and British Emancipators. (*War Illustrated*, 2 June 1917, p.349)

Arthur Roberts was born in Bristol in 1897 of mixed-race parents. His Afro-Caribbean father, David, was a ship's steward. The family moved to Glasgow where the young Arthur was educated at Kent Road School. He remained in full-time education till he was 18 and it is clear from the quality of his prose that he was a highly intelligent and articulate young man – something of a 'dandy' in his style.

1914

One hundred years have passed,
Still the blame goes on,
No black, no white,
No good, no bad,
There stood glory,
There fell fate,
Where was sense,
Where was shame,
We must never forget,
Those who gave,
Their todays,
For our tomorrows, nor those who lived
And bore the scars for life.

Roy Laycock

Arthur took part in a series of battles in the late summer and autumn of 1917, collectively known as the Third Battle of Ypres but more popularly referred to as Passchendaele after the small Belgian township that formed a final objective. Tommies floundered and stumbled forward in an ocean of reeking slime, pouring out their lifeblood in torrents, before the smear of dust which was all that remained was finally taken by the Canadians in November.

PAT AT THE FRONT

An English, Scotch and Irishman
Had once been called upon to plan
A fair division through the three,
Of four fresh eggs laid down for tea.

The Saxon failed and could not show,
Nor did the clever Scotchman know;
'Those two,' said Pat, 'are for you two'
And these there two are for me too.

B.G. Roughead, 12 October 1917

It was not only humans who suffered. Hundreds of thousands of horses, used as cavalry mounts and for the dangerous drudgery of hauling guns and stores, were swept up by the insatiable demands of the frontline. Many animals suffered terribly. Not all were like 'Galloper' Jack Seely's famous charger Warrior, who came home safe.

THE BATTERY HORSE

He whinnied low as I passed by,
It was a pleading sort of cry;
His rider, slain while going back,
Lay huddled on the muddy track.
And he, without a guiding hand,
Had strayed out on the boggy land;
And held there by the treacherous mire,
Lay exposed to shrapnel fire.

He was a wiry chestnut steed,
A type of good Australian breed;
Perhaps on steep Monaro's height,
He'd followed in the wild steer's flight,
Or out beyond the great divide
Roamed free where salt bush plains are wide.
Or, through the golden wattle groves
Had rounded up the sheep in droves,
Then shipped away to feed the guns,
And help the boys to strafe the Huns.

His load was eighteen pounder shells,
The sort that in a barrage tells.
I drew the shells from out their sheath
And cut his girth from underneath,
Then lifted off his saddle pack
To ease the weight and free his back.

His muzzle softly nosed my hand
Because I seemed to understand.
My steel hat from an old time trench
I filled three times his thirst to quench;
I brought my ration biscuits back,
And fed him from my haversack.

No horse that had been stable fed
More proudly tossed his chestnut head
Because a stranger saw his need,
And, passing stayed to give him feed.
But time pressed on, I must not stay,
Four weary miles before me lay.
He made a gallant bid to rise,
Then sank with almost human sighs;
I hoped a team might see his plight,
And draw him out before the night.

Now you may ask, why in this strife
When times were grim and death was rife
I should have ventured from my course
To try and help a battery horse?
I'll tell you why, I felt his need,
I've owned and loved a chestnut steed.

Lance-Corporal E.R. Henry

Even the humble mule, a workaday poor relation of the gallant steed, had his admirers:

O mule with voice so shrill and hide so hard
We've always thought you were strictly barred,
From classy cavalry
Just now you are content
But when your shoes get bent
And to the forge you're sent
There'll be some revelry!

Plum & Apple, October 1915

Besides there was always relief in grousing (complaining), the soldier's universal balm:

THE ORDERLY OFFICER

When at the stables you're kept slaving
And the day is cussed hot
The horses are ill-tempered
And the Sergeants swear a lot
Don't curse the British Army
Or sing the hymn of hate
Just strafe the orderly officer
For keeping you so late!

Plum & Apple

THE WATTLE, IVY AND GUM

The leaves you sent across the sea,
They brought a breath of home to me;
I felt that with the three leaved spray,
That in each leaf a season lay.
The golden wattle's bloom so rare,
Brought golden youth to do and dare,
Australia's best to write their name,
Upon the priceless lists of fame.

The rose of England cannot vie
With wattle blooms when our men die.
The ivy leaf appears to me,
It breathes of a tenacity,
And bids us hold what we have won,
And cling on till the war is done.
The old gum tree was built to last,
And weather many a wintry blast.

So we against the foe must stand,
For liberty and our homeland.
Each comrade wears a talisman,
To bring him luck, if luck it can,
Some wear a rosary of beads,
To help them on to noble deeds,
And some a cross, that Providence
May slay an evil consequence.

Some portraits of their girls divine
With eyes like stars and lips like wine,
Who may for those across the foam,
Prefer the man who stays at home.
All I had on was my old disk,
To show who fell and took the risk.

But now I wear a bunch of leaves,
Fresh from the land where my heart cleaves;
And should a foeman cross my track,
And if his steel should force me back,
To find a way and make the room,
He'll have to crush the wattle bloom;
And cut the clinging ivy strand,
With strong and no uncertain hand;
But if he breaks the old gum tree,
Why, then, of course, he'll conquer me.

E.R.H., *On a Gift of Leaves*

1914–18: HOME FRONT

May Clarissa Gillington Byron (a relative by marriage of the famous poet) is best known as the abridger of J.M. Barrie's *Peter Pan*. Indeed, she came up with the title, *Peter Pan and Wendy*. She was the author of over a hundred books of biography, children's fiction, cookery and verse. Her poems also appeared regularly in newspapers. She is less often credited as one of the inspirations for James Joyce's *Ulysses* – the Irishman was very taken by the structure of her biography, *A Day with Shakespeare*.

Her Irish father was chaplain at Brookwood Asylum in Surrey where she grew up. Fifty-three when war broke out in 1914, she still sounds strikingly modern, displaying a mix of humour, sharp intelligence and a robust sensibility to the realities of life. Her 1913 poem 'At Bay' reads like a harbinger of the conflict to come, while the introduction to *May Byron's Ration Book* puts many a twenty-first-century food faddist to shame.

AT BAY

My child is mine.
Blood of my blood, flesh of my flesh is he,
Rocked on my breast and nurtured at my knee
Fed with sweet thoughts 'ere ever he drew breath,
Wrested in battle through the gates of death.
With passionate patience is my treasure hoarded,
And all my pain with priceless joys rewarded.

My child is mine.
Yet all his grey forefathers of the past
Challenge the possession: they o'er cast
His soul's clear purity with dregs and lees
Of vile unknown ancestral impulses:
And viewless hands from shadowing regions groping
With dim negation frustrate all my hoping.

My child is mine.
By what black fate, what ultimate doom accursed,
Shall be that radiant certainty reversed?
Tho' hell should thrust its fiery gulfs between,
Tho' all the heaven of heavens should intervene
Bound with a bond not God himself will sever.
The babe I bore is mine for ever and ever.
My child is mine!

May Byron, 1913

From her 1918 Ration Book, Preliminary Remarks:

I am not going to minimise the difficulties which lie in wait for the rationed housewife. The making of bricks without straw is notoriously a hard job; and the concocting of palatable dishes with a deficiency of those ingredients which we were wont to use so freely, Is not at all an easy task. No amount of imagination will make baked haricots the least bit like roast mutton. No extent of make-believe will turn vegetable stock into good beef gravy. The question of nutriment is one thing, that of texture and taste quite another. Of course, professional optimists will say it is very good for you not to have this, that or the other; they will chill your blood by talk of proteins and calories and carbohydrates, and will declare that all you really need for health is to be found in split peas and sago. I have even seen tapioca recommended as a substitute for fat! But nobody ever yet tried to fry potatoes in tapioca.

Never a thrifty nation, we have dwelt for half a century in a fools' paradise, believing that 'to-morrow shall be as this day and much more abundant'. Now, when faced with the crude incontrovertible fact that we live on an island and that nearly all our food has been coming from outside that island, there is no doubt that the present rude awakening should – in the long run – be very much to our advantage. 'It's an ill wind that blows nobody good'. To begin with, a fools' paradise is a weakening and demoralising habitation; to go on with, we are now compelled, willy-nilly, to learn the use and value of expedients, of substitutes, of skilful cookery – in a word, of brains. I conjecture that, sooner or later, we shall emerge from this dire emergency a great deal cleverer than we were before; having acquired all sorts of knowledge, and exploited all manner of possibilities, which we should have regarded with a stare of blank bewilderment in 1913.

May Byron was right to point out that civilian life was altered by the war, creating an environment that felt strange to many returning soldiers. Rather like the hero of Sebastian Faulks' classic Birdsong, who experiences a sense of dislocation when he goes on leave, civilian life had continued largely unaltered whilst the soldiers life was changed forever. Yet, at the same time, his experiences have become the stuff of that most popular form of entertainment – the cinema.

THRILLING RAILWAY FILM AT THE EMPIRE CINEMA

A thrilling adventure on the railway and a stirring story of love and hate were amongst the film dramas exhibited at the Empire Cinema. The love story was 'A Fight to the Death' telling of two sailors struggling for a French girl's hand, filmed in a mock realistic manner, and, in 'The Broken Circuit' was seen the miraculous escape of Helen, a popular cinema actress, after she had been tied to the rails in front of an oncoming train. 'Out of the Storm' was a western subject, concerning a hold-up and an exciting capture.

HER SWEETHEART'S DOUBLE

That a bride can marry a counterfeit presentment of the man who she is expected to wed is something to wonder at and yet the spectacle of this being accomplished was convincingly depicted on the screen at the Newcastle Picture House, Grey Street, yesterday in a film named 'The Best Man'.

'The Miser's Daughter' presented a pretty romance, and a very interesting subject was 'Meal Time of the Birds'. There was a big array of comedies of a thoroughly enjoyable type and also a good supply of war films.

Illustrated Chronicle, 6 April 1915

Waste Not, Want Not (leaflet produced by the National Food Economy League/
authors' collection)

THE WAR FILMS

O living pictures of the dead,
O songs without a sound,
O fellowship whose phantom tread
Hallows a phantom ground –
How in a gleam have these revealed
The faith we had not found.
We have sought God in a cloudy Heaven,
We have passed by God on earth:
His seven sins and his sorrows seven,
His way worn mood and mirth,
Like a ragged cloak have hid from us
The secret of his birth.

Brother of men, when now I see
The lads go forth in line,
Thou knowest my heart is hungry in me
As for thy bread and wine;
Thou knowest my heart is bowed in me
To take their death for mine.

Henry Newbolt, 1916

And of course, there was Music Hall:

The French clown, Grock, and his partner in musical novelties, will provide the chief attraction at the South Shields Empire, next week. In addition, a strong company is billed, including The Four Swifts, in their clever club-juggling act; the Richardini Troupe, in a display of physical culture; Dale and O'Malley, the entertainers; H.O. Wills, 'the Water Rat', and others.

MYSTIFIED AUDIENCES

There is a very happy programme at the Pavilion Theatre, Newcastle this week; the mysteries of Giordano, the Italian illusionist, keep the house in a state of perplexity all the time this resourceful 'magician' occupies the stage, and the applause accorded his efforts is spontaneous and hearty. Charlie Bell and company supply a very laughable interlude in the 'The Demon Photographer' and Frank J. Parker and assistant have a remarkably smart turn in 'An Athlete at the Club'.

The Hara Truim, the originator of a skilful clog tango, furnish a very pleasing act and there are also enjoyable items by Master George Warren, whose refined musical act is well worth a visit to the Westgate Road hall; O'Wray and O'Dare, eccentric burlesque comedians; Enid Browne, vocalist; and Dalston and Lane, Hebrew patter comedians.

Illustrated Chronicle, 14 July 1915

Not all casualties were sustained at the Front, however. The pain and suffering could come closer to home:

D.L.I. PRIVATE OF SPENNYMOOR DIES AT BIRTLEY WITH RAZOR IN HIS HAND

Private Edward Charlton Wilkinson, 37 years of age, 6th D.L.I. stationed at Durham died yesterday afternoon as a result of serious injuries to his throat. The man's home address is 2 Dobson's Buildings, Low Spennymoor where are his wife and four children.

Yesterday afternoon, a youth named Harold Oyston ... heard someone groaning. He searched and found Wilkinson lying on the roadside. His throat was cut almost from ear to ear and he was bleeding to death very rapidly.

An open razor was found clasped in the dead man's hand. He has been absent from his regiment since June 19th.

Illustrated Chronicle, 1 July 1915

Allied propaganda stressing the brutality of the German invasion of Belgium had an effect. 'The Dutiful Son' cartoon (*Illustrated Chronicle*, 3 April 1915) shows a fat German sitting in his underwear. Two German men in uniform, one a general, are saying to each other: 'Papa is sad. Let's make him laugh quickly. General, give orders for some bombs to be dropped on women and children.'

Most churches, whilst anxious not to condone the spilling of blood, had actively supported the war from the pulpit, many vociferously. The *Illustrated Chronicle* from Monday 5 April 1915 reported:

In his monthly letter to the Diocese, the Bishop of Birmingham pleads for restraint in the treatment of German pirates.

'We cannot cease our efforts,' he writes, 'till we have accomplished our work; but we shall continue to fight as gentlemen, though our opponents may use the methods of assassins. It is this feeling which makes me so anxious that we should treat even such of our prisoners as have been engaged in what we think piracy and unworthy work with restraint.

'It is not that I do not underrate the longing to wreak vengeance upon those who have done dirty work, but I confess I dislike the rather gloating way in which some people suggest that the men who have been engaged upon the so-called German "blockade" should be treated and tried when captured as felons.'

'NOW WHO'S GOING TO BE FIRST?'

The Man from the Front Does Some Straight Talking to the 'Shirkers'.

I edged my way into the crowd. A tall, sunburnt soldier was talking quietly in serious tones. He leaned over a raised desk with his stick in his hands. A Union Jack hung from a pole by his side. He was sparing of gesture.

The homely image was the weapon, upon which he relied, with a word or two of slang for ornaments, says the Westminster Gazette. Latin's dead. He had no tricks – the words came from the living mouth – he had looked into hell. He was calling for recruits and spoke of men who hung back, 'shirkers' shouted a woman.

Well, that's one word for 'em – I've heard worse than that though. Oh! Haven't they got any imagination? I'm sure if they could but see the sights I've seen they'd come rolling up – aye, rolling up – wreck and ruin wherever you look – fire and brimstone all that there – dead and living all mixed up of a heap ... Then you'd feel what I feel. Just one bang of his great fist on the desk ...

Then a band came marching by with a crowd behind it and the roll of the drums made our flesh creep.

But the music only raised his scorn and bitter ire. He paused. The strains died away.

Yes! It's all right when the band plays – it sounds fine, don't it? Makes you want to knock somebody down – like when you see the soldiers at the Picture Palace and they plays 'Rule Britannia' on the pianny – then you wave yer hats and handkerchiefs and give 'em a cheer.

Oh! yes, I know – like when you sit at home by the fire with your slippers on, (there's no slippers in the trenches – you never get your boots off – there's lots o' fire though) and read the fine stories in the papers – and then you say, 'We've done well today'.

We've done well! Like that – we've done well – and those are the men who stop comfortably at home and pinch the jobs of them as is *fightin' the battles for 'em – pinch their jobs – aye! They'd pinch the missus if she'd let 'em – [a general roar of laughter].*

'Not me,' shouted a woman, 'and he's left five little 'uns behind 'im' – one in her arms.

'We'll take care of him,' said the soldier gravely ...

Illustrated Chronicle, 3 July 1915

FOUND ON THE FIELD OF BATTLE IN FLANDERS

Seven photos, three of them found together, show three children and a man in uniform. We have a group of young people out of doors – some sort of outing perhaps, two girls pictured together with 'From Isa' written on the back and a middle-aged woman sitting with a man in uniform standing beside her. The text states:

'We have received several photographs which have been picked up on the field of battle and we are publishing them in the hope that the owners will be discovered. Some of those which have been already claimed will be sacred memorials of brave local soldiers in future years. And, indeed, in the cases where the owners return to their homes once more they will be valuable mementoes of the Great War. On June 22nd we published three photographs which had been found in the trenches by Pte. A. F. Clarke, 9th D.L.I., of Gateshead and two of them have already been claimed. The curious coincidence is that Gunner T. Slater, R.F.A. [Royal Field Artillery], of Gateshead, recognised his own portrait in the "I.C. [Illustrated Chronicle]" whilst lying in a Newcastle hospital. This he had given to Corporal. D. Horton, 9th D.L.I., of Gateshead, who was slightly gassed, but has since returned to the firing line.

Beneath the photos is the legend, "Found by a Faithful Durham".'

Illustrated Chronicle, 14 July 1915

Doing Her Bit. (*War Illustrated*, 4 August 1917, p.1)

ZEPPELIN RAIDS

JOSEPH COWEN

OF
STELLA HALL, BLAYDON-ON-TYNE
WILL PRESENT
£500
TO THE
CREW OF THE FIRST AIRCRAFT
TO BRING DOWN
A GERMAN ZEPPELIN
IN THE
BRITISH ISLES
OR
BRITISH TERRITORIAL WATERS

Full page ad in the *Illustrated Chronicle*, 5 July 1915

Lascelles Abercrombie was one of the Dymock poets – a group who lived in or near Dymock in Gloucestershire from 1911–14. Fellow members and friends included Ivor Gurney, Robert Frost, Rupert Brooke and Eleanor Farjeon. Abercrombie was born in Ashton upon Mersey, not far from Manchester, in 1881. He began writing poetry in 1901 while earning his living working as a clerk in a Liverpool quantity surveyor's office run by a family friend. Eventually able to survive as a freelance journalist, he wrote poetic drama as well as verse.

Deemed unfit for military service, he moved back to Liverpool in 1916 to work in a munitions factory. Abercrombie was amongst the last people Rupert Brooke wrote to from his sickbed, a mere three weeks before his death. It is surely a testament to their professional and personal relationship that Brooke bequeathed royalties from his published work to Abercrombie; an income which helped to sustain him through the war years.

After the Armistice, Abercrombie was to become Professor of Poetry at Leeds and Reader at Oxford University. In 1931 he gave the oration when a memorial statue to Brooke was unveiled on the island of Skyros. A year later he wrote of their time at Dymock:

> *I have lived in a cottage in the daffodil country, and I have, for a time, done what I wanted to do ... and I have known what it is to have Wilfrid Gibson and Robert Frost for my neighbours; and John Drinkwater, Rupert Brooke, Edward Thomas, Will Davies, Bob Trevelyan, Arthur Ransome, have drunk my cider, and talked in my garden. I make no cider now, and I have no garden. But once I lived in Gloucestershire.*

Abercrombie died in 1938 at the age of 60.

Written as a play in idiomatic verse form and published in 1922, 'The Deserter' is the story of Martha and her nameless lover. Martha has just been widowed, only to discover that her alcoholic husband has left her deeply in debt to the scheming Luther, who is quite open about his plans to coerce her into marriage by exercising emotional and financial control over her and her daughter. During their conversation we learn that Martha is attracted to a soldier friend of her husband who has gone off to fight in France.

[Martha goes to the door of an outhouse opens it and peers in.]

MARTHA: *Sound asleep, poor boy! He said he'd had to walk most of the way.*

[She goes in and shortly after comes out with a young soldier.]

MARTHA: *Well and what if they do see? You're on leave.*
SOLDIER: *I'm not.*
MARTHA: *Then how … ?*

SOLDIER: *You said I had to come.*
                There is no leave: we're going out.
                I mean they are.
                I'm a deserter.
MARTHA: *What's the right name for me, I wonder?*
SOLDIER: *Nay, they won't touch you.*
                You made me do it, but it's me that did it;
                And it is me they'll lag.
MARTHA: *We'll get round that; you'll see.*
SOLDIER: *And how will I get round it, Martha?*
                Can you see that?
                They're going out, and I deserted.
                Well? You said I had to come.
                Nobody ever gave a woman aught that cost the same as this!

> But let that be.
> It was for you.

MARTHA: O, but for both of us!
And we will put it right.
We'll put all right; there's a deal more than this.
But you don't know.
We're safe now.

SOLDIER: Where is a deserter safe?

[break]

MARTHA: You don't see, I suppose, I've made myself all yours?
SOLDIER: O Martha, was there any need to shame me?
He's gone the staggering sot who fleered between us;
could we not wait?
MARTHA: No! Do you want me still?
SOLDIER: Well, I've deserted for you:
I've sneaked off,
Cringing away from men who were my sworn friends,
Just when the danger's sighted.
Don't I know how, when their talk happens upon my
name,
They'll spit it out as if they tasted dirt!
And you say do I want you?
I wish I didn't!
MARTHA: You've done this for me.
Now there's more to do.
And if it were ten times worse than what you've done
I'd ask you for it.
SOLDIER: I'll be bound you would; and I suppose I'd do it.
MARTHA: You'd have to do it.
You don't know what the work's been here, while I
have been alone,
And you've been smartly soldiering.
You don't know what it is to feel the chance of what

may happen to you,
Like a live thing watching you – sitting there quietly,
with bright eyes
Smouldering like a fiend's, hungering at you,
Crouched there waiting, set like the spring of a trap,
Eyeing the strain you make to keep away;
And still you are pushed sidling nearer and nearer;
Until it comes to him, the panther's moment,
To leap and hug me against his loathsome breath!

[break]

SOLDIER: *That's not a way to talk.*
             And do you mean you've brought me here with my
             brain buzzing the word like clockwork ...
MARTHA: *What word?*
SOLDIER: *Deserter, deserter!*
             Whatever I hear now, there'll be that word in it!
             And all because an old blackguardly man shows he
             has a mind to marry you.
             Why, it's a joke.
MARTHA: *I'm in his hands like – but you'll think that silly:*
             Only it is so; as long as I stay here.
             He needs no more than breathe – and all I am,
             All that my life knows for its very own,
             Would scatter like flighty down. But I'll try this.
             There was a story in the papers: how a woman was
             walking in the tropics by herself,
             And one of those huge monkeys carried her off.
             They got her back; she said, as the beast came close,
             Snarling with pleasure to be handling her,
             The life in her stood fixed: her flesh set hard
             As grit stone at his twitching fondling paws.

[break]

SOLDIER: *There's more in this than I can well make out.*

MARTHA: *More than anyone can: let it alone.*
You've come; that's the main thing. Don't make it now
All for nothing! Take me away from here!
Marry me; make me your own property
Nobody else can touch – then, what you please:
Everything after that is all yours, yours.
But away from here, away from here!

SOLDIER: *All right,*
Since you have got me here, I may as well
Go through.

[break]

SOLDIER: *You needn't go on telling me; I believe you.*
I had the choice of being a passable man
Or a swindling sneak-thief, lily-livered deserter.
I've chosen as you asked me; and why not
Go on that way? It will not harm me now.

MARTHA: *Why, but you talk as though I only take,*
And cannot give.

SOLDIER: *Well, that's how it is, it seems.*
I am not grumbling. What is there you can give?
It's been a cruel price, and I'm right glad
It's been all mine to pay.

MARTHA: *O I am sure*
This will be rankling soon.

SOLDIER: *You're hard to please.*
I've paid the shot for both of us, and make
No grudge of it.

MARTHA: *Then we start out of tune,*
And you will come to hate me.

SOLDIER: *Have I not proved*
I love you? Have I not made myself for you,

A thing I loathe? What is it now you want?
Am I to cheer about it?

[break]

SOLDIER: *What made him die?*
MARTHA: *The neighbours say it was*
             The way he drank: he'd sooner drink than live.
SOLDIER: *Do you say that?*
MARTHA: *I know he wished to live.*
             O horribly he wished to go on living!
SOLDIER: *And yet his demon made him kill himself!*
MARTHA: *Yes. I was his demon. There had to be an end!*
             And Luther always strolling by the house,
             Pleasantly scanning around at crops and meadows,
             But never a flicker of looking for me, as though
             He past a thing here too familiarly
             His own, to bother with a glance at it!
             There had to be an end! – And with you here!
             Well, I have done it. Is this not giving something?
SOLDIER: *My God! What have you given me? A murder;*
             You killed him?
MARTHA: *Nobody could call it murder.*
             I let him kill himself.
SOLDIER: *He did not want to die:*
             You were just saying so.
MARTHA: *That's true; it was*
             A thing so hideous, I wonder I don't laugh
             To think of it; longing to live he was;
             And whimpering to himself to stop, he'd reach
             To grope if there were liquor handy – O,
             The bottle was always there!
SOLDIER: *Where you put it.*
MARTHA: *There were two things. Peter would take his time,*
             A month, six months, how should I know? – And die.

You'd be in France, and I'd go down alive
Into the filth of hell: O I have felt
As if to flay myself where Luther's touched me
Would make me laugh like a child at being tickled,
If it would take the sickening sense of him off me!
That was one thing I saw. And there was this –
Peter might die before you went to France,
And very soon you would be going, you said.
You'd come for me; and I need not be the pleasure
Of a fiendish monkey, if Peter would die soon.

SOLDIER: And so you plied him.

MARTHA: I tell you, you can't blame me.
He'd promised me to Luther. And what great thing
Is a dram more or less to a dying tippler?

SOLDIER: I am not blaming you; but I am going.

MARTHA: Going? Where to?

SOLDIER: The way I came. I know
What I shall have there; it's clean black or white,
The offer there: you live or else you're killed.
But here well, I can say this for the war:
It does get you away from living at home.

MARTHA: I've killed your love for me.

SOLDIER: I can't tell you.
When I'm in clink, and feel a decent man,
I shall know that. Now all I know is this –
I will not let the life that you belong to
Touch me.

MARTHA: So I should soil you!

SOLDIER: It's no good,
Martha, A man's not dainty if there are things
He cannot eat.

MARTHA: You are not really going?
O leave love out! For pity's sake –

SOLDIER: I can't!

MARTHA: You will let Luther put his clutch on me?

SOLDIER: *You'll have me weakening; I must go now.*
                I should feel safe if I could see the bayonets,
                Coming to take me and likely I'll meet them.

[He goes]

Morley Roberts (1857–1942) was the son of a tax inspector and became famous as the author of over eighty books and novels. He was born in London and educated in Bedford and Manchester. He took a steerage passage to Australia in 1876 and spent the next three years working in a variety of manual jobs on sheep stations and elsewhere. This was to be the pattern of his life over a number of years as he acquired a body of experience to be used as fuel for his writing.

HER SON IN WESTMINSTER GAZETTE

My baby boy, he was so sweet,
From curly head to rosy feet;
My honey that was most of me.

I made him grow, I let him be,
He was a little king to me;
He ruled my heart and all my brain.

He yearned to be a man and gain
Great glory, though he knew my pain,
And pressed my hand and stroked my head.

He has the glory and is dead.
And I have tears I must not shed:
My honey, honey who is dead ,
That I made live and caused to be,
My boy who was the most of me.

Morley Roberts, 1918

6

1918: VICTORY

The final year of the war was very nearly the end for the Allies. With Russia prostrate, the German High Command could move over a hundred divisions – battle hardened and trained in new infantry tactics – westwards. The *Kaiserschlacht* battles of spring and early summer would see the Allies pushed back and ever backwards, ceding more ground than had shifted throughout the war, but never broken.

NEVER MIND

If your sleeping place is damp,
Never mind!
If you wake up with a cramp,
Never mind!
If your trench should fall in some
Fill your ears and make you dumb
While the sergeant drinks your rum,
Never mind!

If you have to rise at four,
Never mind!
If the morning's dark and raw,
Never mind!
If a duck-board should elope
And your container has no rope,
And you have to wade and grope,
Never mind!

If the cook's a trifle new
Never mind!
If you get your tea and stew
All combined,
And you find your pint of rice
Has a coat of muddy ice
Try to think it blanky nice,
Never mind!

Anon.

Tommy was tested as never before, pushed back to the gates of Amiens and, in Flanders, to the walls of Ypres. Haig uttered his 'backs to the wall' order, and backs to the wall it was. Tommy came through the crisis of the battle, but again at fearful cost:

> *Who was the wag, who during a weary march in file from the ramparts to the trenches, passed back the message; 'Last man shut the Menin Gate?'*

Walking Out. (Drawing in autograph book, 1914–18, author's own)

'*Tout le monde a la bataille,*' cried Marshal Ferdinand Foch who, in this hour of need, became supreme Allied commander. Germany's great gasps continued but with weakening frequency and the Americans were arriving.

THE LONE PINE CHARGE

The boys of the First Brigade stood to their arms;
From the lines of the foeman rang out the alarms.
We crouched as we waited the shrill whistle blast,
Each knew that his effort might well be his last.
The signal rang out and we sprang to the work,
With bayonets in line and each face to the Turk;
And we thought every gun in the universe talked,
As the reaper, grim death, took his toll as he stalked.
The wounded fell prone, ne'er again would they rise,
For the shrapnel sowed death as it rained from the skies
But the remnant pushed on and came up with the Turk,
Great gaps in their ranks but in stern mood for work,
Some Turks stood their ground – there were some who had fled.
But we harried them well and the trenches ran red,
They plied us with shot and the dread hand grenade.
Yet slowly, but surely our progress we made.
For six days and nights raged the battle apace,
And each showed the other the dash of his race.
But a silence crept over the trenches one night,
And we knew when it deepened, that we owned the fight.
Not a hand grenade thrown – not a shot from a gun
We breathed for a space – Lone Pine had been won.

Anon.

Afterward, enjoying victor's laurels, Foch would write:

> *War requires an ingenious mind, always alert, and one day the reward of victory comes. Don't talk to me about glory, beauty, enthusiasm. They are verbal manifestations. Nothing exists except facts and facts alone are of any use. A useful fact, and one that satisfied me, was the signing of the armistice … Without trying to drag in miracles just because clear vision is vouchsafed to a man, because afterwards it turns out this clear vision has determined movements fraught with enormous consequences in a formidable war, I still hold that this clear vision comes from a Providential force, in the hands of which one is an instrument, and that the victorious decision emanates from above, by the higher and Divine will.*

In a war marked by filth, squalor, constant attrition and a vast, unceasing haemorrhage of broken and maimed, 'the knights of the air' seemed outwardly to represent something nobler, more Homeric than mass slaughter on the ground. This was a fiction, of course – propaganda on both sides. War in the air was every bit as deadly.

ALL THE BOYS WANT TO BE AIRMEN

The 'boy airman' is the most wonderful of all the wonderful combatants in this war. Those in authority like to catch him young, for his 'nerve' is better and he comes into training as an absolute stranger to fear. Shortly before the war an angry parent called in on his boy's schoolmaster, 'I don't know what to do with my boy,' he said despairingly. 'All I can get out of him is that he wishes he were a bird and could fly.'

'Well,' replied the schoolmaster, 'if the war comes we shall want all the human birds we can get hold of. Let him fly.' So the angry parent reluctantly 'let him fly'.

Three months after his training was finished, the boy came to see me. He had turned into a man, as the old lady put in 'an eye like a hawk'. He was in truth a human bird and told me of the dangers he had passed as coolly as if he were narrating the incidents of a football match. The second time he came, his face was disfigured by two of the most awful black eyes I have ever seen on any human countenance. 'How did it happen?' I asked. 'Oh,' he said, in a matter of fact tone, 'I was making a turn and didn't put enough back into it, it's just like a side slip on a bicycle.'

'And you came down?'

'Of course I came down!'

'And did the machine come down too?'

'There wasn't any of it left in workable shape. A week in hospital put me alright.'

G.B. Burgin

In fact, the average life expectancy of a rookie flyer was just six weeks; in combat this could easily be measured in minutes.

COMMAND OF THE AIR

A thousand years between the sun and sea
Britannia held her court of liberty,
And cradled heroes in the questing waves
That were for lesser men but wandering graves.

Then did the British airman's sea-born skill
Teach wood and metal to foresee his will;
In every cog and joint his spirit stirred;
The Thing possessed was man as well as bird.

A falcon among timorous fowl he flies,
And bears Britannia's battle to the skies;
Vainly the Hun seeks covert in a cloud
The clinging mist is made his ghostly shroud.

Thus at the ringing gates of heaven's glory
Begin new chapters of our island-story,
And clarion voices of the void declare:
'She who has ruled the sea shall rule the air.'

Anon.

LA BELLE FRANCE

The Boy stood in the ... (pardon) trench
As he was paid to do;
The life was ensanglante* (French for bloody)
The pay was one and two
And even that (if he might mention it) was overdue.

The mud was thick as you could find;
Its quality was such
As shops would call 'a special kind,
Most yielding to the touch'
He tried, but could not call to mind
Things he disliked as much.

He did not pat his diaphragm
Nor wave his handkerchief,
At sight of food. He gave no damn
(This passes all belief)
For Yuletide plum and apple jam,
For Christmas bully beef.

Explosive shells were overhead,
Do, mines were underneath,
'My Goodness,' more than once he said,
'This is a blasted heath'
He meant thereby that he was fed
Up to his backmost teeth.

Anon.

A better fortune than fighting. (Author's own)

By mid-summer the German offensives had finally run completely out of steam. Now it was Haig's turn. General Ludendorff would describe 8 August 1918 as the 'Black Day' of the German Army. The British, finally fighting an all-arms co-ordinated battle, punched through at Amiens. There was no rout, never a sign of collapse, but the writing was very much on the wall. From now on during the 'Hundred Days', every step the Kaiser's men took would be backwards. Tommy might feel a little more cheerful:

Thou shalt not covet thy neighbour's wife,
His ass though shalt not slaughter
But thank the Lord it is no crime
To covet another man's daughter!

R.L. Morley, Royal Naval Air Service

MY LITTLE DRY HOME IN THE WEST

I've a little wet home in a trench
And the rainstorms continually drench
There's the sky overhead, clay or mud for a bed
And stone we use as a bench
Bully beef and hard biscuits we chew
It seems years since we tasted a stew
Shells crackle and scare, yet no place can compare
With my little wet home in the trench

Anon.

George Purvis' younger brother, Stanley, whose vocation after the war led him into the ranks of the clergy, wrote regularly to his mother from the Front. His letters were expanded into a regular press column, 'The Life of Our Soldiers', under the pseudonym of Orion. These features were a bridge between those at home and those in the line. Stanley's particular talent was to make sense of the whole situation by using recognisable and homely images, guiding his East Riding readers around the intricacies of trench systems:

TRENCH SYSTEMS

Probably all the trenches that you have seen yourselves are those dug along the cliffs for practice. They will give you many wrong ideas. In the first place these trenches have never been under fire and perhaps out here we should have little use for trenches dug that way. What you cannot realise from seeing trenches at home is that the trenches in France are part of an enormous system. Let me attempt a familiar illustration;

We will forget for a moment that Yorkshire has a sea coast. You and I, dear reader, are going to our front line. We pass along St. John's Street which unfortunately has suffered much from the enemy's heavy shelling. We avoid High Street because it is shelled regularly all the way along up to the ruins of the Bayle Gate and the Priory, so we turn instead along South Back lane. Here we find a shallow trench running along one edge of the road and out into the fields beyond and as the enemy can observe this spot from balloons we enter the trench and proceed along it.

A battery of our guns is firing below the shelter of the bank in Well Lane; the gunners have their dugout under the ruins of the rectory. A few yards further on the trench crosses the road which is pitted with shell-holes and then runs along parallel to the way to Boynton. The motor signs at the cross roads are still standing but perforated and scarred by shell splinters. The trench passes the mound of bricks which used to be Rose Cottage (flowers in the garden continue to flourish in the midst of ruin) and then strikes off a little up the hill to the right.

Now and again you catch glimpses of similar long trenches cutting the slope on the other side of the valley, one above and one below the much battered Wandale Farm; a trench which comes out from the wood on the hilltop on that side cuts right across the valley and joins our trench ... At every junction the trenches are carefully labelled; Oxford Street, High Street, Beck Alley, North Trench, Boynton Abbey, and they are all much used.

The woods have been greatly thinned by bombardments. At least half the trees are down and the remainder slashed and splintered by shells. The timber is utilised for building dugouts, repairing the trenches or for firewood. The trenches now become an absolute maze ... they branch and cross in all directions in the most confusing way. Some of them are in good repair and regular use; some abandoned and falling in.

I have omitted the thousands of guns, machine guns and trench mortars, all in their emplacements, of dugouts and shelters, strong-points, observation posts and numberless other features of trench life.

Tommies' humour remained proverbial. It had to be, for the horrors of war could not be contained by fine sentiments, and these soon tarnished. For every Graves, Sassoon or Wilfred Owen, there were a thousand others, less elevated or less bitterly reflective:

BE IN THE FASHION

Why have cats, dogs, canaries, rabbits, parrots etc.

LICE!

Every conceivable shade supplied – blue backs, black backs, red backs, grey backs, white backs; also in a delicate pink shade and with variegated stripes; pure thoroughbreds from our own seams, most clinging, affectionate and taking ways; very prolific, hardy and will live anywhere. Once you have them you will never be without.

In dainty pochettes at 2s per thousand!

Even the deadly art of the sniper, which came fully of age during the war, did not escape humour:

> *FOO [Forward Observation Officer]: Is this the best way to trench 31?*
> *Jock Sniper: Yes, you go doon the 'Y' communication trench till ye come*
> *to the wee hoose and when you get past the wee hoose, you want to mind*
> *your 'Ps' & 'Qs', as they've got a machine-gun on it, and keep your*
> *stern up an' yer heid doon so if ye do get one, it's a Blighty one!*

'Blighty' remained an ideal, though many found once there they could only think of getting back to the line, so greatly had their perspectives been altered.

GETTING BACK

I've heard men say when in the camp,
Or on the sea or on the tramp,
The tales they'll tell to folks at home
If they win through and cross the foam
And get safe back.

Some carry with them day and night,
A souvenir of some big fight,
To show to friends where they have fought,
On fields where victory's dearly bought –
If they get back.

While thunderous cannon rend the skies,
They face the foe with steady eyes;
Though some get through, there's some must go,
Who try conclusions with the foe,
All can't get back.

Our boys who fell have left a name
Upon the priceless lists of fame;
The memory of those brave hearts dear,
All I ask is a souvenir,
If I get back.

Lance-Corporal E.R. Henry

Tennyson's summation of the Charge of the Light Brigade was echoed in 1918: 'Into the mouth of Hell' – the Western Front was a parallel war. Whilst millions burrowed beneath what had been fields and lanes to make trenches, others dug far deeper. As trench lines hardened, as troops became used to this static, submerged existence, both sides sought to gain advantage by digging under the other's lines. This became a new dimension of conflict; miles of subterranean galleries, partly defensive to intercept the enemy, and partly offensive. Mines packed with explosives would be detonated under key bastions in the enemy line to clear the attackers' path.

Sir John Norton-Griffiths, better known to imperial and Great War contemporaries as 'Empire Jack' or 'Hell-Fire Jack', had served in the Matabele and Second Boer Wars. He became a successful engineer and, in 1914, raised a volunteer battalion at his own expense and was promoted to major. Norton-Griffiths was the Tommy's Marshal Vauban (a brilliant military engineer famed for his skill in designing fortifications and breaking through them), directing the construction of fortifications all along the line which he toured in a Rolls-Royce, suitably equipped with a first-rate travelling cellar.

He gives us an exchange of memoranda concerning the high explosive ammonal; even the underground war had its humourists:

TO 5TH CORPS HQ

Can you please say if you have made use of any ammonal and, if so, whether the results are satisfactory?
  Signed, Lieutenant-Colonel G.F. Farmer etc.

TO CAMP COMMANDANT, 5TH CORPS

For report please.
  Signed, Lieutenant-Colonel W.H. James etc.

TO AG & QMG, 5TH CORPS

This is not understood. For what purposes is ammonal used please? Is it a drug or an explosive?

Signed, Lieutenant-Colonel J. Fryer etc.

TO CAMP COMMANDANT, 5TH CORPS

Perhaps the medical officer attached to Corps HQ will be able to give you all required information?

Signed, Lieutenant-Colonel W.H. James etc.

TO AG & QMG, 5TH CORPS

In accordance with your previous minute, I have consulted the MO in command of 5th Corps HQ. He informs me that ammonal is a compound drug extensively used in America as a sexual sedative in cases of abnormal sexual excitement. So far as I am able to ascertain, this drug is not in issue to Corps HQ. Under the circumstances, I regret that I am unable to report as to the results of the use of ammonal being satisfactory or not and, at the present moment, the MO states that no cases have occurred among 5th Corps HQ personnel indicating the necessity for administering the drug.

Signed, Lieutenant-Colonel J. Fryer etc.

FOR SALE

A desirable villa situated in Vermelles;
Ideal for anyone fond of fresh air;
Every inconvenience;
Latest War news;
Battlefield attached.

Plum & Apple, 1918

There would be a pacifist reaction in the post-war era, though conscientious objectors, or 'Conchies', had a rough ride during the conflict itself:

TO A CONSCIENTIOUS OBJECTOR

You'd leave me cold though this our arguing
Endured till dawn, you lack the essential thing.
Healthy and leisured, pious, gentle, learned,
'You feel forbidden to fight' and thus unconcerned
With that vast horror which defeat would bring.

Hence, tho' you touched of David's lyre the string,
Or wrote with quill plucked from an angel's wing,
Unless you 'gave your body to be burned',
You'd leave me cold.

'You feel it wrong to nurse'. While others fling
Red life in the scale, what is your offering?
Levite! In you the milk of pity has turned!
For if sore wounded, and with eyes that yearned,
I lay in the Jericho Road a-perishing,
You'd leave me cold!

H.M.W., 30 December 1916

A generation of young women would be blighted: lovers, fathers, husbands, brothers, all taken:

WAITING

I wanted to beg you to stay; instead I smoothed my apron and watched you walk away.
I wanted to fall down on my knees and cry and scream and plead and plead and plead,
Instead I boiled water, made tea while you fastened braces, polished boots, shone buttons.

'I'm more likely to die down that bloody pit,' you said, we both knew it wasn't true.

'This is our way out, our chance to get away, from the grime and the dirt and the same places/faces day after day.'

You always thought you were better than our little town, where we grew up side by side,
Always the tallest, strongest, fastest and bravest lad at school: born for better things.

I knew you all my life, loved you since we were fifteen, and now I had to say goodbye.

'It's not for long love,' you said, 'we will all be home by Christmas love.' You kissed me, held my gaze with those blue, blue eyes and turned and walked away.

I held that image in my mind till this day, you striding down the street, proud to be in khaki, prouder still of the red cap covering your sandy blond hair.

Played it over and over in my mind over the years, wondered if I
could have changed things in anyway
Sixty five years to the day I watched you stroll down our street round
the corner, gone.

I'm old now Johnny, and now at last, I hope, soon, to see you again.

Samantha Kelly

War correspondent Philip Gibbs reported in his bulletin to the
North Mail on 12 November:

Our troops knew early this morning that the armistice had been
signed. I stopped on my way to Mons outside a Brigade HQ, and
an officer said 'hostilities will cease at eleven o'clock'. Then he
added as all men add in their hearts, 'Thank God for that'. All the
way to Mons there were columns of troops on the march and their
bands played ahead of them and almost every man had a flag on his
rifle. There were flowers in their caps and in their tunics, red and
white chrysanthemums given by crowds of people who cheered them
on their way, people who, in many of these villages had been only
one day liberated from the German yoke. Our men marched singing
with a smiling light in their eyes. They had done their job and it was
finished – with the greatest victory in the world.

It was a victory, one dearly bought and one which led inexorably to an even worse war within a generation. That this was 'the war to end all wars' proved a bitter irony. The harshness of Versailles and Germany's shame would open the door for Hitler and the Nazis. Tommy would not return to 'a land fit for heroes'. They came back to poverty, unemployment, hunger and despair. Their sons were forced to march again twenty years later.

POPPIES

We glory not in war
We long for peace
But we remember those
Whose lives were lost striving to gain that peace.

Each generation seeks an answer
To the curse of war,
But anger, greed and inhumanity
Rule in hearts of men
And hopes of love and brotherhood
Are scattered like the dust.

We wear our poppies – be they white or red –
As symbols, not of triumphing in glories past,
Of celebrating warfare and old victories,
But from respect for those who died,
And tokens of our deep desire
For world-wide peace –
Red and white prayers for wars to cease!

Jennifer Laidler, May 2009

Through all the land, in city, town, village and shire, the sad memorials rose; a mournful roll call of the lost, a hymn to a lost generation. Yet all too soon, other names were added from the next war and are added yet.

THE LAST WORD; FROM CHARLES MOSS

Sir,

I wonder how many of the lads who volunteered as I did during the golden autumn of 1914 still remain to talk over the pleasures and rigours and discipline of those intensive training periods? One of them has just had the poignant experience of revisiting the well-remembered localities around Salisbury Plain and, for the moment, to shed the weight of the years and wounds, as memory brought back those boisterous and hard-driven days.

In our spare time, when not on parade or manoeuvres we busied ourselves by cutting copies of our regimental cap badges through the turf, giving each one a setting as white as that of the famous horse. It was a moment of deep emotion when this old Durham Pal came after forty-five years and found so many of the badges clear and well-tended.

Those who had lived through that war of foul trenches, wiring patrols and attacks over No-Man's-Land which were the dire and hellish responsibility of the PBI [Poor Bloody Infantry], could forget those grand autumn days of 1915 when they gathered juicy blackberries as big as cherries from the tall hedges and munched apples dropped on the road from overladen trees.

Durham Advertiser, 10 November 1961

Finis

Sources

Introduction

The words of Charles Moss are from his memoir, reproduced by kind permission of Durham County Record Office (DCRO); 'To Germany' is from Osborn, E.B. (ed.), *The Muse in Arms* (John Murray, 1917); 'Victory Day' is from *The Queen's Gift Book – In Aid of Queen Mary's Convalescent Auxiliary Hospitals* (c.1920); 'No Conscription' by kind courtesy of the Trustees of the Green Howards Museum; 'Release' and 'Racing Rhymes' are from Osborn, E.B. (ed.), *The Muse in Arms* (John Murray, 1917).

Chapter 1. 1914: Expectation

'Shall We Forget Them' appeared in the *Daily Mail* in August 1927 and is here shown by kind courtesy of the Trustees of the Green Howards Museum (Green Howards); 'The Noodles and Rifleman's Dispute' and the following quote are taken from Hewitson, T.L., *Weekend Warriors from Tyne to Tweed* (Tempus, Stroud, 2006); 'Spirit of the New Army' – authors; 'I vill send out Ultimatums' is reproduced by kind courtesy of Tyne and Wear Archives and Museums (TWAM); 'The Call of the Pipes' is from Stewart G. and J. Sheen, *Tyneside Scottish* (Pen & Sword, Barnsley, 1999). All quotations from

the Waugh Memoir are by kind courtesy of the Trustees of the
Fusiliers Museum of Northumberland (Northumberland Fusiliers);
'Wor Contemptible Little Army' and 'The Big Push' are repro-
duced with the permission of TWAM; Stanley Purvis' sermon is
reproduced by permission of the Green Howards, as is 'The Bonny
English Rose'; Field Marshal Haig is quoted in Ellis, J., *Eye Deep in Hell*
(Crook Helm, London, 1976); 'The Bold King's Hussars' appears
by permission of the Trustees of the Northumberland Hussars and
TWAM, as do all quotes from the unofficial journal of the Hussars.
Further quotes on the winter of 1914 are from the regimental history of the Northumberland Hussars; 'Hints for Tommy from one
wot knows' – authors; 'Battle of the Falkland Islands' and 'Guns
at Sea' are from Osborn, E.B. (ed.), *The Muse in Arms* (John Murray,
1917); 'A Shanty of the Emden' is from Newbolt, Henry, St Georges
Day (John Murray, 1918); 'The Kaiser's Night Soliloquy' is from the
Illustrated Chronicle (21 August 1915); 'The Iron Cross' is from *The Echo
and Evening Chronicle* (3 April 1915). Both of the latter by kind permission of Newcastle Libraries.

Chapter 2. 1915: Resignation

'Release', 'Light after Darkness' and 'Domum' are from Osborn,
E.B. (ed.), *The Muse in Arms* (John Murray, 1917); 'Come Ye Apart,
Be Still' is from the *Illustrated Chronicle* (April 1915) by kind permission of Newcastle Libraries; 'The Second Battle of Ypres' and
'The Road' are reproduced by kind permission of DCRO; Extracts
from *Plum & Apple* are included with the permission of TWAM; the
poem beginning 'We've served with you etc.' was written about
Lieutenant James Barker Bradford of the remarkable Bradford
brothers, two of whom won the VC – neither they nor James sur-
vived the war; Extracts from Lieutenant Gamble's letters and verse
are also included with permission from DCRO; 'Ypres' is another
taken from the Queen's Gift Book; 'The Things that Matter' and
'Ilium' are also reproduced with the kind permission of DCRO.

Chapter 3. 1916: Death

'Puzzled' is reproduced by permission of the Green Howards; Private Gill's doggerel is from the authors' collection; Stanley Purvis' words again from the Green Howards; 'The Tyneside Scottish at the Battle of the Somme' is by permission of TWAM; Charles Moss again appears by permission of DCRO; Private Glenn's doggerel appears by kind permission of Northumberland County Record Office (NCRO); The ode discovered by Moss and comrades appears by permission of DCRO; Private Wiles' contribution – authors; 'Unofficial Orders' are reproduced with permission from NCRO; 'The Soldier's Bride' by DCRO; 'Outposts' is from Osborn, E.B. (ed.), *The Muse in Arms* (John Murray, 1917); 'Close of Play' is from Ashley, K.H., *Up Hill and Down Dale* (John Lane, 1924).

Chapter 4. 1917: Mud

'Kitchener's Army Soldiers Christmas Day in the Workhouse' is reproduced by kind permission of DCRO; 'Heroes of Home' is from the Green Howards, as is Captain George Purvis' correspondence; Lieutenant Terry's prose and verse are by kind permission of the Northumberland Fusiliers; 'Tommy Atkins' appears by kind permission of DCRO; The verse by Arthur Roberts appears by kind permission of Morag Miller and family; 'Pat at the Front' – authors; 'The Battery Horse' and 'On a Gift of Leaves' is from DCRO; the ode to a mule (*Plum & Apple*) and 'The Orderly Officer' are from TWAM.

Chapter 5. 1914–18: Home Front

'At Bay' is from the *Poverty Bay Herald* (22 February 1913); 'Preliminary Remarks' is from *May Byron's Rations Book* (Hodder, 1918) by kind permission of the Library of the Literary & Philosophical Society of Newcastle upon Tyne; 'Thrilling Railway Film at the Empire Cinema', 'Her Sweetheart's Double', 'Mystified Audiences' and the 'music hall review' are from the *Illustrated Chronicle* (6 April 1915 and 14 July 1915) and courtesy of Newcastle Libraries; 'The War Films' is from Newbolt, Henry, *St Georges Day* (John Murray, 1918); the extract from the report about Private Wilkinson is from the *Illustrated Chronicle*, as is the item about the Bishop of Birmingham's Letter (1 July 1915 and 6 April 1915, respectively); 'Now Who's Talking', 'The Dutiful Son', 'Found on the Field of Battle in Flanders' and 'Zeppelin Raids' are from the same source (3 July 1915, 14 July 1915 and 5 July 1915) and are by kind permission of Newcastle Libraries; 'The Deserter' is from Abercrombie, L., *The Poems of Lascelles Abercombie* (OUP, 1930), with thanks to the Library of the Literary & Philosophical Society of Newcastle upon Tyne; the extract from his letter comes from the Friends of the Dymock Poets website at www.dymockpoets.co.uk; 'Her Son' comes from the *Westminster Gazette* (21 August 1915).

Chapter 6. 1918: Victory

'Never Mind' is from DCRO, as are 'The Lone Pine Charge', 'All the Boys want to be Airmen' and 'La Belle France', and the dog-gerel by R.L. Morley RNAS; 'My Little Dry Home in the West', together with Stanley Purvis' prose, is included by kind permission of the Green Howards; *Command of the Air* comes from Osborn, E.B. (ed.), *The Muse in Arms* (John Murray, 1917); 'Getting Back' appears by kind permission of DCRO; Major Norton-Griffith's observations appear by kind courtesy of the Royal Engineers Museum and Archive; Doggerel from *Plum & Apple* is included by kind permission of TWAM; 'Who' is from the authors' collection; 'To a Conscientious Objector' is included by courtesy of DCRO; 'Waiting' is original verse by Samantha Kelly, as is 'Poppies' by Jennifer Laidler.

Every effort has been made to trace copyright holders. The authors and publishers would be pleased to hear from anyone who feels they have been missed out.